An Insider's Guide to Working for the Federal Government

T0289716

ALSO BY DAN LINDNER

A Guide to Federal Contracting
A Guide to Defense Contracting

An Insider's Guide to Working for the Federal Government

Navigating All Levels of Government as a Civil Servant or Contractor

Dan Lindner

Bernan Press

Lanham • Boulder • New York • London

Published by Bernan Press
An imprint of The Rowman & Littlefield Publishing Group, Inc.
4501 Forbes Boulevard, Suite 200, Lanham, Maryland 20706
www.rowman.com
800-865-3457; info@bernan.com

6 Tinworth Street, London SE11 5AL, United Kingdom

ISBN: 978-1-64143-402-7
E-ISBN: 978-1-64143-403-4

Contents

Preface

While writing two reference books on contracting with the federal government, I reflected on a number of events which I experienced during my career of nearly 40 years in and supporting the federal government. It struck me that there were sufficient anecdotes, events, and lessons learned to write a separate volume to demonstrate to the general public what it is like within the halls of the federal government. Numerous biographies written by and about presidents, cabinet secretaries, and military leaders reveal what happens at the top levels of government, but little is available regarding the daily workings of government at the operational level. This book is intended to provide such a discussion—to reveal what the day-to-day life of a bureaucrat is really like and how the machinery of the federal government really works. Both civil service and the contractor community are addressed herein, along with anecdotes of events that occurred in my career. I have collected 100 lessons learned from my career, which are liberally sprinkled throughout the text in the form of suggested rules of behavior and approach to the job.

Some readers may be encouraged to work for the government, either as civil servant or contractor. Others will at least learn a bit about this business, how it works, and what it means to America. But all readers will be affected in some way by the content.

I've kept acronyms to a minimum, including only those frequently used in the profession. I've spelled them out where first used. References to a personal position, such as (s)he, are used to avoid any bias. The term (sub) contractor is used whenever a concept applies equally to both prime and subcontractor. For brevity, I use the term *agency* to signify both departments and agencies. Likewise, *office* is used to describe an individual work component, regardless of its name in reality.

Many people have contributed to my success through my years of experience as a federal contracting officer, project manager, and analyst. I have been blessed to work with countless professionals who provided their guidance and wisdom, especially Marie Flynn, Dave Brickley, John Dunegan, Jim Sharpe, Graham Wright, Frank Ford, Grey Cammack, and Elliott Branch of the Department of the Navy. From the Department of Defense came the talents of Bob Donatuti and Bob Long. Similarly, I am grateful to Hugh Hosford, Ed Traccarella, Paul Robert, and Norm Brown for their legal counsel, all first-rate civil servants. The experiences I obtained with several interagency working groups were invaluable in learning much and meeting many. On a personal note, my greatest thanks go to my wife Jennie and our sons Eric and Alex for their support.

—Dan Lindner

Chapter 1

The Tricameral Form of Government

In the spring of 1787, a group of prominent American gentlemen met in Philadelphia to address shortcomings of the confederation government then in existence. The confederation consisted of a congress where each state had co-equal status regardless of population, a couple of clerks to carry out their statutes, no national currency, an empty treasury, and an inability to handle disputes between states. The gentlemen decided right away that the confederation approach was not working and instead crafted an alternative form of government. Among the numerous issues that they wrestled with, the desire to separate the legislative, executive, and judicial powers of government was addressed and quickly resolved. They invoked the ideas promulgated by the French jurist and philosopher Charles-Louis de Secondat, Baron de La Brède et de Montesquieu, who argued that these three powers must be assigned to three separate branches of government. In *The Spirit of Laws* (1748), he wrote:[1]

> When the legislative and executive powers are united in the same person, or in the same body of magistrates, there can be no liberty; because apprehensions may arise, lest the same monarch or senate should enact tyrannical laws, to execute them in a tyrannical manner.
>
> Again, there is no liberty if the judiciary power be not separated from the legislative and executive. Were it joined with the legislative, the life and liberty of the subject would be exposed to arbitrary control; for the judge would be then the legislator. Were it joined to the executive power, the judge might behave with violence and oppression.

Hence, our Founding Fathers created a tripartite form of government. We have a congress to enact laws, a president to implement them, and a

---

1. Montesquieu, *Complete Works, Vol. 1 (The Spirit of Laws)*, Book XI Chapter VI.

court system to enforce and interpret them. This approach provides a series of checks and balances on power, such that no one branch can thoroughly dominate the political agenda and operations. Such an arrangement tends to moderate the ambitions and power of actors in the political arena, thereby frustrating any attempts to create autocracy.

Each branch has numerous employees to carry out their assigned functions. Let us look at each branch in turn.

JUDICIAL BRANCH

The judicial branch of the federal government is the easiest to understand. It comprises the federal courts which adjudicate all cases involving alleged violations of federal law. They also handle lawsuits alleging actions which violate the letter and spirit of the Constitution. Within the executive branch, there are thousands of lawyers to address these issues, thereby leaving the balance of civil servants to focus on their daily duties. There are three levels of federal courts:

- district and special courts,
- the Circuit Courts of Appeals, and
- The Supreme Court.

The nation's district courts are the trial courts for most matters of federal jurisdiction. These courts resolve disputes by determining the facts and applying legal principles to resolve the dispute fairly and impartially. Each state has at least one district court, and large states have as many as four. In total, there are 89 district courts in the 50 states, plus one in the District of Columbia and another in the Commonwealth of Puerto Rico. Three other U.S. territories also have courts that hear federal cases: Guam, the Northern Mariana Islands, and the Virgin Islands. Note that American Samoa does not host a federal court, so their federal cases are normally heard in Hawaii.

There are also several courts with specific jurisdictions. The Court of International Trade has jurisdiction over any civil action against the United States arising from federal laws governing import transactions. This includes classification and valuation cases, and can review certain agency determinations under the Trade Agreements Act of 1979 involving antidumping and countervailing duties.[2] In addition, it has exclusive jurisdiction of civil actions to review eligibility determinations of communities, firms, and laborers under

---

2. Office of the Law Revision Council, House of Representatives, United States Code (U.S.C.) 2501.

the Trade Act of 1974.[3] Civil actions initiated by the U.S. government to recover customs duties or debts on a customs bond, or for certain civil penalties alleging fraud or negligence, are also within its exclusive jurisdiction. This court is based in New York City.

Another special court covers appeals from the U.S. Court of Appeals for the Armed Forces of military court-martial convictions. Despite its apparent military nature, this court is civilian in nature, residing in downtown Washington, D.C. This approach frees such appeals from any military command or influence. This court applies constitutional principles to members of the armed forces to review appealed convictions.

The U.S. Court of Federal Claims is spread throughout the nation to hear cases involving claims of monetary judgments against the U.S. government. Such claims can arise out of many activities, such as:[4]

- bid protests,
- civilian or military pay,
- congressional actions such as private bills enacted to benefit a specific party(ies),
- contracts,
- excise taxes,
- Indian affairs,
- patents and copyrights,
- *takings* (federal regulations which limit the use of private property), and
- vaccine injury.

The United States Tax Court sits in Washington, D.C., and hears cases specifically involving federal income taxes. This is where taxpayers and firms go when they object to an income tax debt imposed by the Internal Revenue Service.

One other special court in Washington, D.C., is the U.S. Court of Appeals for Veterans Claims. This body focuses on decisions by the Board of Veterans Appeals concerning veterans' disabilities and pension and survivor benefits. It also hears cases concerning dependent educational assistance.

On the next higher level, we have eleven Circuit Courts of Appeals designed to cover multistate geographic areas. There is also a dedicated circuit for the District of Columbia and another for the Tax Court. These appellate courts hear appeals from decisions of the District Courts and the special

---

3. 19 U.S.C. 2101.
4. United States Court of Federal Claims, "Frequently Asked Questions."

courts mentioned above.[5] The Circuit Courts of Appeals also hear appeals from final decisions of the:

- agencies' boards of contract appeals;
- discrimination claims of presidential appointees or congressional employees;
- International Trade Commission;
- Merit Systems Protection Board; and
- secretaries of the various departments.

These issues need not go to a district court, but rather may go directly to the regional Circuit Court of Appeals.

The highest court of the land is the Supreme Court of the United States. Over the course of a term, more than 7,000 petitions are filed for cases to be briefed before the Supreme Court, though only one percent are actually heard.[6] Moreover, each year, about 1,200 applications are filed that can be acted upon by a single justice while serving in the capacity of a circuit justice. The Supreme Court is also the original and sole court of jurisdiction for cases involving multiple states (such as border disputes). An example is when the states of New Jersey and New York disputed who owned the land where the Statue of Liberty is located; the Supreme Court voted in favor of New Jersey. The Supreme Court also has the option to hear cases involving the federal government against a state, and ambassadors from foreign nations.[7] Decisions by a majority of the Supreme Court members are considered to be final and binding on all.

LEGISLATIVE BRANCH

Article I, Section 8, paragraph 18 of the Constitution gives Congress the authority to enact laws to implement federal powers. The Constitutional Convention was highlighted by a great debate between the large states who objected to the confederation model of an equal number of delegates from each state and the smaller states who wanted their voices heard rather than drowned out by the larger states. A compromise was needed and became established in our national legislature model.

---

5. However, the Circuit Courts do not hear appeals of decisions handed down by the U.S. Court of Appeals for the Armed Forces. Appeals from this court are rare, usually for a death sentence or refusal to hear a case or issue a writ on appeal, but would go directly to the U.S. Supreme Court.

6. General Services Administration, "How the Supreme Court Works."

7. 28 U.S.C. 1251(a) and (b).

As a result of this debate, Congress contains two separate chambers. The *House of Representatives* has 435 members allocated based on population across the country, so long as each state has at least one dedicated member.[8] This distribution is revised every ten years (when the number of the year ends in a 2) after the latest census data is released. The *Senate* contains two members from each state regardless of its population, for a total of 100 members.

This idea of two senators for each state was developed during constitutional deliberations to ensure that all states are treated equally. However, this means that even the smallest state with just one representative has a total of three elected members of Congress and thus three votes. According to the apportionment of representatives derived from census data, there are seven states that have only one representative.[9] The arithmetic tells us that seven out of 50 delegations (14 percent) receive the minimum number of congressional representatives, which has no bearing on population. Based on 2019 census projections, the United States has a total population of about 330 million.[10] The smallest states have a total population of roughly 5.6 million according to the same data. Based on these numbers, we can see that 14 percent of the elected Congress represents only about 1.7 percent of the population. This is the quantitative argument against the current system. However, any change would require a constitutional amendment, which will be difficult to adopt when the small states vote to reject the amendment.

Congressional representatives and senators have their own *personal staff* members who are personally selected based on shared ideology and loyalty rather than individual merit. Obtaining a staff position is somewhat like applying to a law firm—the best way to do so is to have an inside or influential contact. New hires sometimes obtain their positions after volunteering in the legislator's campaign or serving as an unpaid intern to obtain contacts for finding a permanent job. Most new hires, however, come straight out of college (often majoring in political science or communications), starry-eyed that they will work in the center of legislative power. They quickly learn that the pace is very hectic and their tasks are very mundane, such as:

- answering telephones,
- dealing with lobbyists,
- drafting letters in response to constituent communications that are either off-the-wall or embarrassing to their boss,
- listening to angry constituents,

---

8. Cohen and Barnes, *The Almanac of American Politics.*

9. U.S. Census Bureau, "Apportionment of the U.S. House of Representatives Based on the 2010 Census." The one-member states are Alaska, Delaware, Montana, North Dakota, South Dakota, Vermont, and Wyoming.

10. U.S. Census Bureau, "US States—Ranked by Population 2019."

- making coffee and fetching food from the cafeteria,
- running papers to other offices,
- tolerating elected officials who sometimes exhibit selfish and totalitarian attitudes,
- watching senior staff and committee members do all the policy research, and
- working late into the night.

Because their pay is modest (often about $30,000), the vast majority of staffers are under age 40. Coupled with long hours, burnout is widespread and turnover is high (the average tenure is only two or three years).[11] The prime directive among staffers is to make their boss look good—always. And of course, their job only lasts so long as their boss is in office—a lost election means a lost job! Remember that representatives only serve for two years until they must stand for re-election, so the long-term job survival rate by personal staff members is not always good.

Both chambers have *standing committees* with staff members who are also selected based to some extent on political ideology. These committees and their subcommittees number about 200 in total. Bills are considered and hearings are held in committee, although a great deal of negotiating is done informally between elected officials and their staff members. The elected officials send out mailings postage-free to their constituents to inform them on current issues and legislation (and hopefully not on their reelection campaign, which would be illegal, although the line can get blurry).

Committee staff members bear significant differences from most personal staff aides. This is where legislation is written and significant policy and legal research is performed. Individual staff members often become experts in a limited number of issues (unlike the generalist nature of personal staff work). There are actually two sets of staff members on nearly all committees, one for the majority party and the other for the minority party.[12] The draft legislation is taken up in committee hearings, line-by-line, word-by-word, and revised and massaged until a majority position is reached among committee members. Turnover is much lower on committee staffs, with longevity of five years quite common. Many committee staff members later obtain senior appointive positions within the executive branch as a result of political contacts made on committee work. However, one important simi-

---

11. The total number of employees on Capitol Hill is hard to determine, but the total number of staff aides is somewhere around 14,000. See https://www.legbranch.org/2016-6-17-how-many-congressional-staff-are-there.

12. Exceptions may exist on the House and Senate Judiciary Committees, where the chairman and ranking minority member sometimes opt to consolidate their committee staff members.

larity with personal staff work is the need to summarize complex material into understandable writings.

Both the House and the Senate have an Office of Legislative Counsel, a nonpartisan group of attorneys who draft legislation and ensure it complies with current federal law and accurately reflects the desired policy. The hours are not as onerous for this group and political influences are not necessarily required. Congress is also responsible for the Architect of the Capital and the United States Botanic Garden and has its own police force. But there are several other offices managed by Congress that are of significant interest.

The *Library of Congress* serves both legislative staff and the general public with a collection of over 100 million publications.[13] This collection contains books, magazines, manuscripts, maps, newspapers, photographs, pamphlets, and recordings on every subject and in every conceivable language.[14] The manuscript collections include the personal papers of many presidents prior to Herbert Hoover, who was the first to establish his own presidential library (as has every president since). Its positions are civil service rather than political in nature, so there is much greater job security and no personal allegiance to elected officials. It also contains the Congressional Research Service to provide a wide range of policy and legal research services to the legislators and their staff members.

The *Congressional Budget Office* (*CBO*) provides research on budget preparation and related economic issues. CBO assists the congressional budget committees with drafting and enforcing the annual budget resolution. CBO then analyzes the proposals set forth in the president's budget request and details the impacts of alternative spending and revenue options, comparing them to their most recent spending and revenue target projections. Upon committee request, the CBO also analyzes and reports on specific policy and program issues which have budgetary impact. The CBO provides cost estimates of every committee-approved bill to show how it would affect spending or revenues over the next five or ten years, depending on the type of spending involved. These estimates include the impact on state, local, and tribal governments as well as on the private sector. Each year, the CBO issues reports on the federal budget and economic outlook for the next ten years. Unlike committee and personal staffs, CBO is a nonpartisan office which does not make policy recommendations and identifies all underlying assumptions and methods in its reports. As a result, CBO analyses and reports bear a high level of credibility.

---

13. On a personal note, I am proud to say that both of my previous books are available in the Library of Congress.

14. Yes, Trekkies, they even have some material written in the Klingon language!

The *Government Printing Office (GPO)* produces and distributes official publications for all three branches of the federal government. Employing about 1,700 people, GPO also authenticates, catalogs, preserves, and disseminates the official information products in both digital and paper forms. GPO prints both the *Congressional Record* of deliberations in Congress and the *Federal Register*, a legal information service of the U.S. government to publish administrative regulations and notices, federal laws, and presidential documents. Both of these publications are produced at the main plant; however, GPO contracts most of its printing orders to thousands of private vendors across America. GPO not only sells its products to the general public, but also distributes them to federal depository libraries and on its www.govinfo.gov website.

The *Government Accountability Office (GAO)* reviews fiscal performance of operations in all three branches by means of financial and performance audits, investigations, policy analyses, and program reviews. It gathers information for Congress to determine how effectively executive branch agencies are carrying out their missions, especially in terms of meeting their objectives and providing services of value to the public. It audits agency operations, investigates allegations of illegal and improper activities, and issues legal decisions and opinions (often through reports from the general public via its FraudNet hotline program). Its reports, often called *blue books*, help members of Congress better understand emerging, long-term issues. GAO also refers criminal allegations to appropriate law enforcement and inspector general offices. Their database contains report recommendations that still need to be addressed and is available to the general public. GAO also hears protests by bidders on federal contracts in its role as fiscal watchdog and has the power to stop a procurement action if it finds that the government is not fairly conducting the bidding or negotiation process. In this role, they act as a referee to ensure the government is following the rules in source selection. This office of nearly 2,000 analysts produces roughly 900 reports each year, usually in response to a specific request from one or more legislators. These reports receive high visibility among government officials and program managers, and occasionally appear in the newspapers if the subject matter is interesting or titillating.

EXECUTIVE BRANCH

Article II, Section 3, Clause 4, requires the president to "take care that the laws are faithfully executed." When the nation first began this tripartite scheme in 1789, there were only a few dozen people needed to do so. Today however, the multitude of laws and programs requires dozens of departments and agencies. Nearly one million Americans now serve in the armed forces and another million support them as Department of Defense (hereafter referred as DoD) civilians. Adding another two million civil servants in all other departments and agencies yields a total payroll of four million (more or less) jobs in the executive branch alone![15] Needless to say, this creates a multitude of employment opportunities.

The *executive branch* primarily consists of three different types of organizations: the Executive Office of the President, departments, and independent agencies. We will look at the latter two in the next chapter.

The *Executive Office* includes the president's and vice president's personal staffs, which are largely political in nature, and serve at the pleasure of the president (or vice president). We have seen the nature of their work in fictional television dramas such as *Designated Survivor* and *West Wing*, which are actually fairly accurate in presenting how these staff members work. Dedication to the president is paramount for these people and their length of employment is tenuous at best (they can be hired, fired, or promoted at any time). More than 400 people work within the West Wing of the White House.

Including the several offices within the Executive Office of the President, the total employment is roughly 1,800 people. They create policy in all sorts of domestic areas such as drug control, the economy, environment, national security, and science and technology. They also help the president carry out the political issues and activities on the president's agenda. These organizations work next to the White House in the Executive Office Buildings (there are actually two of these buildings). Let's look briefly at each office within the executive office of the president:

- The Council of Economic Advisers analyzes the national economy to make objective quantitative research and reports to the president.
- The Council on Environmental Quality develops national policies and initiatives to improve the environment.
- The Domestic Policy Council oversees development and implementation of the president's domestic policy agenda and coordinates among the heads of relevant federal offices and agencies.
- The National Economic Council coordinates and advises the president on economic policy to ensure consistency with stated goals and full implementation.
- The National Security Council advises and assists the president to integrate all aspects of national security policy—domestic, economic, foreign, intelligence, and military.

---

15. The current estimate for civilian employment in the executive branch is around 2.1 million. See Congressional Research Service, "Federal Workforce Statistics Sources: OPM and OMB," 6.

- The Office of Administration provides all the usual office management support functions for the entire Executive Office of the President: facilities, internet, library, research, mail, messenger, personnel, printing, and procurement services.
- The Office of E-Government and Information Technology houses the Chief Information Officer of the Federal Government and directs efforts to provide citizen access to federal information resources over the Internet.
- The Office of Federal Financial Management strives to improve federal financial records and systems to reduce improper payments and improve real property accountability.
- The Office of Information and Regulatory Affairs issues policies regarding information, regulations, and statistics.
- The Office of National Drug Control Policy helps the president establish drug control objectives and policies and provides budget, policy, and program recommendations.
- The Office of Performance and Personnel Management helps departments and agencies to develop performance and personnel information and results.
- The Office of Policy Development supports both the Domestic Policy Council and the National Economic Council.
- The Office of Science and Technology Policy provides engineering, scientific, and technological analysis, and opinions on federal plans, policies, and programs, such as economy, environment, foreign relations, health, and national security.
- The United States Trade Representative develops trade policy and directs all trade negotiations of the United States.

Finally, we have the *Office of Management and Budget* (*OMB*). This organization has about 500 employees and is responsible for many functions:[16]

- clear and coordinate departmental advice on proposed legislation and recommend presidential action on enacted legislation;
- consider and prepare proposed executive orders and proclamations;
- coordinate and review regulatory reform proposals;
- coordinate congressional testimony by executive branch officials;
- develop and implement programs for paperwork reduction and public reporting burdens;
- develop ways to coordinate government activities and expand interagency cooperation;
- lead any president-mandated reform or reorganization effort;

---

16. See www.whitehouse.gov/omb.

- oversee agency operations in terms of financing, information technology, personnel, and procurement;
- plan and conduct evaluation of program objectives and performance of the executive departments and agencies and report results to the president;
- plan and develop information systems that provide program performance data;
- prepare the budget and formulate the government's fiscal program;
- promulgate executive orders;
- provide overall direction of procurement policies, regulations, procedures, and forms;
- review the organizational structure and management procedures of the executive branch to ensure that the intended results are achieved; and
- supervise budget administration.

The president can issue *executive orders* to provide operational direction to departments and agencies. The executive branch also issues regulations to implement a statute or Executive Order or policy. These orders and regulations are considered quasi-legislative in nature by federal courts, which give them similar respect without substituting their judgment as to content.[17] Individual agencies are free to develop and implement their own regulations. Regulations are published daily (except holidays and weekends) in the *Federal Register* and formally codified in the *Code of Federal Regulations*. These publications are also available online at www.govinfo.gov, book sales by GPO, and government depository libraries located throughout the nation.

As an office within OMB, the *Office of Federal Procurement Policy* (*OFPP*) assists in revisions to the Federal Acquisition Regulation and develops overarching acquisition policy for the entire federal government.[18] OFPP has issued reports about best procurement practices, workforce development, and contracting out governmental functions.[19] However, OFPP may not always practice a proactive approach, to carefully avoid organizational battles with executive agencies and departments with their own defined jurisdictions and their own tried-and-true methods. For example, I remember early in its existence when OFPP attempted to develop policy on how contractors should pay their labor force. However, the Department of Labor is charged with sole authority to issue labor policies, not OFPP, and angrily appealed to then-President Jimmy Carter to protect their jurisdiction. OFPP backed down and its administrator subsequently resigned. As a

---

17. *Skidmore v. Swift & Co.*, 65 S.Ct. 161, and *American Telephone and Telegraph Co. v. United States*, 57 S.Ct. 170, Government Printing Office, *United States Reports*.

18. OMB is responsible for developing and issuing government-wide guidance on management processes, such as procurement, and to recommend and monitor funding levels.

19. Lindner, *Guide to Federal Contracting*, 36.

result, OFPP has achieved few policy accomplishments of note. Moreover, since its administrator rarely stays on the job more than two years, there has been some talk of converting the position into a career civil service position rather than an appointive office.

All departments and most agencies are headquartered within Washington, D.C., or a few miles outside of it within a highway which loops around the city. This is the infamous *Beltway* or Interstate 495, which runs for 66 miles in a circle around suburban Maryland and Virginia. Since many federal departments and agencies are headquartered "inside the Beltway," the term has come to apply to the federal government leadership, often in a derogatory sense. Critics of the federal government therefore claim that "the real America" lies "outside the Beltway." Ironically, some 85 percent of all federal employees live and work "outside the Beltway."

THE FEDERAL BUDGET PROCESS

To fully understand federal government operations, one must also understand the federal budget process, which is managed by OMB. A *budget* lists all planned expenses and revenues for a given program.[20] A budget can be thought of as a model of how the program might perform financially if certain plans are fully implemented. Management will then measure financial performance against the budgeted forecast to assess performance. The federal budget covers an entire twelve-month period, known as a *fiscal year*. The federal government's fiscal year begins October 1 and expires September 30. Unlike most state governments and private firms, the federal government is allowed to run deficits.

The budgeting process in the federal government is unique and follows a series of individually named steps which are followed one at a time. These steps from budget development to final outlay are basically as follows:

* annual data calls,
* spending plan,
* president's budget,
* budget resolution,
* committee hearings,
* authorization acts,
* appropriation acts,
* apportionment,
* allotment,

---

20. Lindner, *Guide to Federal Contracting*, 60–61.

- commitment,
- obligation, and
- expenditure.

First, the annual U.S. government budget is prepared by OMB, which conducts data calls through all federal departments and agencies and compiles the results. The budget includes a spending plan that shows the state of the Treasury at three different points in time:

- end of last fiscal year (September 30);
- end of current fiscal year; and
- end of upcoming fiscal year.

The president then signs the proposed budget and submits to Congress by the first Monday of February (a deadline which is sometimes missed). Related documents such as the Economic Report of the President are included, along with a description of proposed spending priorities and justifications. This submission is necessary because federal budget authority to enter into financial obligations derives from the Constitution which says, "No money shall be drawn from the Treasury, but in Consequence of Appropriations made by Law . . ."[21] At this point, Congress enters the budgeting process.

Both the House of Representatives and the Senate have Committees on the Budget which draft budget resolutions, usually before the Easter break. These resolutions are then submitted to their respective chambers for consideration and adoption. The two chambers then select members to serve on a conference committee to resolve any differences between the two versions, after which the chambers will vote on the conference version. This resolution may bind Congress, but not the nation, so it does not require presidential approval. Rather, it is a blueprint for the upcoming appropriation process.

Next, congressional committees and staff members hold public hearings and mark-up sessions, and inevitably make numerous substantial changes. Some changes result from legitimate disagreements with the administration over spending priorities and program needs, while others are congressional initiatives resulting from political desires to spend federal dollars on a specific project or initiative.[22] The end result will be a process to authorize and appropriate funds to operate the federal government.

---

21. United States Constitution, Article I, section 9, clause 7.

22. This is also known as *earmarking* or, more colloquially, *pork barrel politics.* The rise of several political movements and the presidential campaign of John McCain, who announced in 2008 that he never practiced it, have spelled the end of this political tradition, at least in theory. However, it is still accomplished under other means to ensure that individual members of Congress look after their constituents, and it remains both perennial and significant.

Unfortunately, these are two separate processes with two separate sets of players. *Authorization* by Congress permits agencies to run programs, but funding is not included. This is because funding for federal programs must first be authorized by an oversight committee for the department or agency concerned. Their deliberations lead to an Authorization Act for the department. These committees have the authority to decide what programs and policies to allow. This also means that the authorization phase comes before the appropriation phase.

Appropriation is the process by which Congress approves funds for specifically authorized programs. Appropriations are set aside by Congress for specific purposes, such as operations and maintenance, procurement, and research and development. However, the Appropriations Committee for each chamber is responsible for "seeing the big picture" of federal operations and is free to make changes to the Authorization Committee decisions. So despite the directions set down in the various authorization acts, the Appropriations Committee of each chamber sets the funding levels, which may not be consistent with the authorization bill. All appropriations must go only to authorized programs, but not all authorized programs may be funded. To add to the confusion, authorizations for some programs may lapse yet still be funded, while other authorized programs may receive no funds at all. Appropriation bills may also contain policy direction, which may or may not coincide with the authorization committee's wishes.

I once came across a civil servant who was a program manager for nine years—on paper. Unfortunately, he never had any money appropriated for his efforts and hence no program to manage. But he was very proud of his title of "program manager" and was free to mention it in his resume, despite never doing anything more than mundane paperwork on a totally different subject. Eventually the agency stopped the charade of proposing his program in the budget when it was clearly unsupported by Congress, and with that went his dream of managing a program.

There are currently 12 appropriation bills enacted each fiscal year, corresponding to the jurisdiction of the respective House and Senate appropriation subcommittees:

- Agriculture;
- Commerce, Justice, and Science;
- Defense;
- Energy and Water;
- Financial Services;
- Homeland Security;
- Interior and Environment;
- Labor, Health and Education;

- Legislative Branch;
- Military Construction and Veterans Affairs;
- State and Foreign Operations; and
- Transportation, Housing, and Urban Development.

Notice that DoD is unique among all departments in that it has two separate appropriation bills: one for construction and housing and one for everything else. This raises the interesting circumstance where one part of DoD is funded on time and the other is delayed. This has happened several times in the past. Generally, military construction is not a controversial subject because Americans want their service members to have decent housing, just like we want to take care of our veterans, so their bill is often approved rather quickly. However, the procurement of weapon programs contained in the Defense Authorization bill may be more controversial and hence delayed in enactment.

Once both chambers of Congress agree on an appropriations bill, it must be signed by the president to become law. The president is free to veto the bill within ten days of arrival, outlining in writing his reasons for veto. Congress may override the veto by a two-thirds margin in each chamber, in which case the bill automatically becomes law without further action. Otherwise, Congress must act to revise the bill to meet the president's objections, propose an alternate approach, and then resubmit the bill to the president.

Each budget item can be classified as either discretionary or direct spending. *Discretionary spending* is an appropriation for a fixed period of time, usually concurrent with the fiscal year. Since these funds must be obligated by September 30, federal contracting offices are under pressure to obligate them by the end of the fiscal year before they expire (hence the term *expiring funds*).

In an alternative vein, *multi-year funding* is specifically granted by Congress for programs they designate that will in fact take more than one year to enact. Congress will make multi-year appropriations for purposes of housing, research and development, and some military systems. This approach reduces administrative burden, broadens the contracting competitive base through higher quantities, lowers costs, and permits continuity of performance or phase-out costs. Alternatively, *no-year funds* assure timely liquidation for acquisition and availability of adequate funds at time of award but are not required to be funded in any specific year.

By contrast to discretionary spending, *direct spending* is enacted by law but not dependent on an annual appropriation bill. This includes most entitlement programs such as Food Stamps, Medicaid, Medicare, and Social Security. It is not normally used to fund federal contracts or salaries.

Once money has been fully appropriated, the executive agencies proceed through several steps to ensure the money goes where intended. *Apportionment* is how OMB provides appropriated funds to the departments and agencies. *Allotment* is how a department divides apportioned funds among its operating divisions. Each division then follows their department guidance to provide funds to the individual program office.

Once funds for federal contracts have been provided to the appropriate office, they must go through yet another lengthy process to get on contract. *Commitment* is the administrative reservation of funds against a future contract, and is done before the procurement package reaches the contracting officer. *Obligations* are funds reserved for payment by the authorized administrative component (e.g., comptroller or accounting authority). *Expenditures* or *outlays* are funds actually disbursed to a contractor for work completed. This will not match the budget authority for the fiscal year because some of the funds can be disbursed in future years, just so they are obligated in the current fiscal year. The program office and contracting officer must take care to ensure that funds are used only for their intended purpose (known colloquially as the *color of money*) to ensure that the directions of Congress are correctly implemented.

The biggest difference between public and private sector accounting is fiscal accountability. A government agency must demonstrate compliance with law and budgetary directives for managing resources. By contrast, the private sector uses budgeting as a planning tool, not as a compliance (and sometimes, not even as a management) tool. Another difference is that the government recognizes revenue when the money is available, not when earned to liquidate liabilities. Similarly, the government records expenses when charged to revenue rather than when incurred.

And what if the budget is not adopted in time? If Congress cannot enact a bill by the end of the fiscal year, a *continuing resolution* may be adopted to continue government operations at the same spending rate as the prior year. If such a resolution is not adopted and signed by the president, the government is theoretically out of business and federal agencies must shut down. This is because the *Anti-Deficiency Act* prevents both the government and its contracting officers from making any commitments without sufficient appropriated funding.[23] Contractors must cease performing against their contracts or else face the prospect of not being reimbursed for their effort.[24] Alternatively, the department may be allowed to spend the funds provided by the continuing resolution at the same pace as in the prior year, or in compliance with additional congressional direction.

As if more bewilderment were necessary, some appropriations bills may be enacted, but not others. It is therefore conceivable that come October 1, some departments may be fully funded and operating as usual, while others

---

23. 31 U.S.C. 1341.
24. This approach is known as *working at risk*.

are either under a continuing resolution or else shut down (or maybe partly closed and partly open). The legislative process is truly a series of multiple power centers, repetitive processes, and endless compromises.

The government is also dependent upon Congress to institute a debt ceiling which limits how much it can borrow to stay in operation. If it reaches the ceiling without an increase by Congress, then it can no longer borrow money and faces a shutdown because it cannot pay its bills. Once again, the Anti-Deficiency Act comes into play. This is a political football which gives Congress another excuse to berate the president for profligate spending, but is always increased because the specter of shutdown is too horrendous to sell to the voters. Most of the public seems to feel that they elected their Congress to enact laws for a functioning government, not to shut it down!

The issue of government shutdowns is sometimes misunderstood throughout America, but certainly not so inside the Beltway. Whenever a budget impasse occurs, or whenever the government reaches its authorized debt ceiling, then in theory the government must shut down. This statement is based on an opinion which President Jimmy Carter requested of his attorney general, Benjamin Civiletti, who said that the Anti-Deficiency Act prohibits the government from any activities other than those otherwise mandated by law.[25] Since Congress has the "power of the purse," civil servants cannot be paid unless appropriations have been made and they must therefore stay home without pay.

If some departments or agencies are funded, then they may continue to operate. During the most recent shutdown in the winter of 2019, four departments were fully funded (including the largest, DoD), so the shutdown only affected about a quarter of federal employees. Yet it attracted nationwide attention as if the government were totally closed.

Shutdowns do not save tax dollars, contrary to popular opinion. Civil servants will eventually get paid and must still complete the work which lay on their desks while at home, often with additional overtime pay. Activities to physically shut down facilities and operations become necessary which would not otherwise occur. Tariffs, park admission fees, and souvenir concession sales revenue are lost. Immigration hearings and legal investigations are preempted. Interest on the national debt continues to pile up and late fees on unpaid bills are added. The GAO estimates that the shutdowns between 2013 and 2019 cost the taxpayers an additional $4 billion.[26] A Senate report confirms this number, based on some 57,000 man-years of lost effort.[27]

---

25. United States Senate Permanent Subcommittee on Investigations, "The True Cost of Government Shutdowns," 10–11.

26. Katz, "Agencies Paid Federal Employees $3.7 Billion Not to Work During Recent Shutdowns," *Government Executive.*

27. United States Senate Permanent Subcommittee on Investigations, 11.

During a shutdown, civil servants of affected departments and agencies are directed to stay home. Unless they are deemed "essential employees" (and those who are essential are told so ahead of time), they must stay home and are legally prohibited from entering their offices. They will not get paid until the shutdown is ended and will probably get their back pay eventually because they are a powerful lobby on Capitol Hill. Moreover, many taxpayers feel they are innocent pawns in this Washington power struggle and must therefore be made right by getting paid. If the shutdown goes for too long, as was the case in the winter of 2019, they may need to file for unemployment benefits with their state government.

Contractors are especially affected by shutdowns. They will never get paid for time lost (under the concept of "no work, no pay"), whereas civil servants have enough of a constituency in Congress that they will receive back pay for time lost. Moreover, civil servants are considered career employees, whereas contract employees are only onboard for a particular project and cut loose whenever their services are no longer required. Contractors don't always have the luxury of transferring their employees to other contracts unaffected by the shutdown, especially if they don't have the requisite security clearance. One contractor executive recently said:[28]

> When your only customer doesn't pay you for nearly four months and you've reached your company's borrowing capacity, you face the dire prospect as a business owner to file for bankruptcy or sell off parts of your business for pennies on the dollar in order to pay your employees. We were within days of having to make that decision.

Companies have unpaid invoices piling up, impeding cash flow and, in turn, delaying vendor payments. Subcontractors have even less room to adjust, since they must wait even longer to get paid from the already-suffering prime contractors. And the loss of revenue can impact the company's ability to borrow funds to tide them over in the short term (or at least raise the interest rate above normal). I had a contractor client whose customer base was entirely within the area impacted by the 2019 shutdown but was lucky to have enough of a credit line to survive and pay its employees. So, the impact of a government shutdown can be inconvenient for civil servants, but especially brutal on contractors.

---

28. Alba Alemán, CEO of Citizant, quoted in Ogrysko, "Federal Contractors Describe 'Insanity and Uncertainty' during Government Shutdown," *Federal News Network*.

Chapter 2

Departments and Agencies

The executive branch employs roughly 2.1 million civil servants.[1] A wide variety of positions and occupations are covered. They include everything from clerks to program managers and support to information systems specialists to intelligence analysts, and the military as well. Many are administrative positions such as program analysts to ensure that the program is on track in terms of performance, schedule, and budget. Others include such positions as

- air traffic controllers,
- attorneys,
- auditors,
- biologists,
- civil engineers,
- correction officers,
- criminal investigators,
- electronics engineers,
- human resources specialists,
- information technology engineers,
- inspectors,
- intelligence analysts,
- logisticians,
- mechanical equipment operators,
- medical care providers (particularly nurses),
- natural resources managers,
- procurement analysts,

---

1. Bureau of Labor Statistics, "Working for the Federal Government: Part I." The United States Postal Service is not included in this number.

- public affairs specialists,
- social workers, and
- veterans claims processors.

There are 15 *departments* within the executive branch. The head of each is named a *secretary* (except the head of the Justice Department who is deemed the attorney general). This term dates back to the early days of our confederation, when the responsibilities of foreign affairs and treasury were largely clerical in nature for our young nation and performed by individuals who sat at secretary desks with the Congress.

Each secretary has a deputy to ensure continuity of leadership due to travel or vacancy. Like the secretary, the deputy secretary is considered a cabinet-level official. Then we have a number of undersecretaries in each department who handle a myriad of policy issues. They are subcabinet level officials who nonetheless require Senate confirmation. Then we have several assistant secretaries in each department, again subcabinet positions which require Senate confirmation. Below that level, to handle operational matters, exist an immense number of officials who do not require Senate confirmation, some of whom are political appointees and some of whom are career civil servants. These include chiefs of staff for each of the above positions, chief information officer, general counsel and inspector general for the department, assistant deputy secretaries, and assistant assistant secretaries, not to mention deputies to all of these officials. Independent agencies are no different—just substitute the word "administrator" or "director" for "secretary."[2]

So why in the world do we have this maze of fancy titles? We don't see this nomenclature quite as crazily in the private sector. Actually, there are several reasons for this. First, the federal government is charged with new duties every year by Congress, so it is growing. When I worked for the Assistant Secretary of the Navy (Research, Development, and Acquisition) for instance, the big issue dominating Capitol Hill was cleaning up the environment (removing toxic waste from our ground and water). So every department was tasked with creating an official (usually an assistant secretary) to focus on this one issue. Of course, this required another set of deputy assistant secretaries and chiefs of staff to actually lead the staff aides in their daily duties and act as gatekeepers for the assistant or undersecretary. Second, every president from Franklin D. Roosevelt to Donald Trump has campaigned about reining in the bureaucracy and tended to implement this idea by bringing in more political appointees to control it! They get fancy titles to reflect both their importance and independence from the competitive civil service. Finally, the

---

2. Office of the Federal Register and Government Printing Office, *The U.S. Government Manual* (2017).

Senior Executive Service faces a pay cap instituted by Congress in response to public objections about their salary levels, so this is a way to give these people a salary commensurate with their responsibilities. Titles are a big deal in Washington, by the way, perhaps more so than in the rest of America.

Of course, this situation presents a problem when it comes to accountability and oversight. These officials have no idea what is happening in day-to-day operations unless they ask for a briefing on the crisis of the day, which is usually introduced by an inquisitive congressional member or news reporter. Then we see a mad scramble among staff aides to find the facts of the issue, draft briefing papers, hold hurried meetings among flustered bureaucrats, revise their briefing papers, and meet with the assistant secretary, who will then meet with the secretary, who then prepares for a hearing on Capitol Hill to present the appearance of being on top of the issue. (S)he really is not, but must appear to be in order to calm down both the American public and Congress and keep it off the backs of the administration and the civil servants.

Each of today's department heads sit in the president's *cabinet* as senior executives and are subject to Senate hearings and confirmation. The departments have somewhat of a pecking order based on date of establishment:

- State (1789)
- Treasury (1789)
- Defense (1947, replacing the Department of War established in 1789)
- Justice (1789)
- Interior (1849)
- Agriculture (1862)
- Commerce (1903)
- Labor (1913)
- Health and Human Services (1953)
- Housing and Urban Development (1965)
- Transportation (1967)
- Energy (1977)
- Education (1979)
- Veterans Affairs (1989)
- Homeland Security (2002)

The Department of State implements foreign policy. It represents the nation and its travelling citizens abroad, coordinates international cooperation on major issues of the day (such as drug trafficking, humanitarian crises, and terrorism), provides foreign aid assistance, promotes foreign export and investment opportunities, and helps combat international crime. The United States maintains diplomatic relations with approximately 180 countries. State includes the following offices:

- Bureau of Arms Control and International Security
- Bureau of Conflict and Stabilization Operations
- Bureau of Counterterrorism
- Bureau of Democracy, Human Rights and Labor
- Bureau of International Narcotics and Law Enforcement Affairs
- Bureau of Population, Refugees and Migration
- Office of Global Criminal Justice
- Office of International Religious Freedom
- Office of the Special Envoy to Monitor and Combat Anti-Semitism
- Office to Monitor and Combat Trafficking in Persons

The Department of the Treasury ensures that our financial system is secure and sound. It produces both coin and currency, issues payments to Americans, collects taxes, and borrows funds to run the government. The Treasury strives to safeguard our financial systems, imposes economic sanctions against foreign threats, and identifies any financial threats to national security. Treasury includes the following organizations:

- Alcohol and Tobacco Tax and Trade Bureau
- Bureau of Engraving & Printing
- Financial Crimes Enforcement Network
- Bureau of the Fiscal Service
- Internal Revenue Service
- Office of the Comptroller of the Currency
- U.S. Mint

The Department of Defense (DoD) provides the military forces to fight wars and protect our security.

DoD is the largest government agency, with more than 1.4 million men and women on active duty (not counting 1.1 million citizens serving in the National Guard and Reserve forces) and over 700,000 civilian personnel.[3] DoD also contains many joint agencies and commands:

- Defense Advanced Research Projects Agency
- Defense Commissary Agency
- Defense Contract Management Agency
- Defense Finance and Accounting Service
- Defense Health Agency
- Defense Information Security Agency
- Defense Intelligence Agency

---

3. Department of Defense, "About the Department of Defense."

- Department of Defense Education Activity
- Defense Logistics Agency
- Defense Security Cooperation Agency
- Defense Security Service
- Defense Threat Reduction Agency
- Joint Improvised Explosive Device Defeat Organization
- Missile Defense Agency
- National Geospatial-Intelligence Agency
- National Security Agency
- United States Special Operations Command
- United States Transportation Command
- Washington Headquarters Services

DoD consists of the Departments of the Army, Navy, and Air Force (the first two were cabinet-level at one time before being consolidated after World War II, although they still retain their "department" titles). They have their own commands and centers:

Department of the Army:

- U.S. Army Materiel Command
- U.S. Army Medical Command
- U.S. Army Corps of Engineers
- National Guard Bureau

Department of the Navy:

- Marine Corps Systems Command
- Military Sealift Command
- Naval Air Systems Command
- Naval Facilities Engineering Command
- Naval Sea Systems Command
- Naval Supply Systems Command
- Office of Naval Research
- Space and Naval Warfare Systems Command
- Strategic Systems Program

Department of the Air Force:

- Air Force Materiel Command
- Air Combat Command
- Air Education and Training Command
- Air Force District of Washington

- Air Force Global Strike Command
- Air Force Intelligence, Surveillance and Reconnaissance Agency
- Air Force Life Cycle Management Center
- Air Force Operational Test and Evaluation Center
- Air Force Reserve Command
- Air Force Space Command
- Air Force Special Operations Command
- Air Mobility Command
- Pacific Air Forces
- Space and Missile Systems Center
- United States Air Force Academy
- United States Air Forces in Europe

The newly created Space Force will undoubtedly generate its own department structure in the future.

The Department of Justice enforces federal laws, combats crime, prosecutes alleged criminals, and imprisons those convicted. As the largest law office in the world, it represents the United States in legal matters, including presenting cases before federal courts and the Supreme Court. It contains several well-known investigative bureaus and runs our federal prisons:

- Bureau of Alcohol, Tobacco and Firearms
- Bureau of Prisons
- Drug Enforcement Agency
- Federal Bureau of Investigation
- U.S. Marshals Service
- U.S. Parole Commission

The Department of the Interior protects our natural resources, including fish and wildlife. This is a huge undertaking, covering roughly 20 percent of our land area. Interior provides recreation opportunities, conducts scientific research, and supports both Native Americans and territorial residents. It also manages mineral deposits and dams and reservoirs. The department raises billions of dollars every year by leasing natural resources such as grazing, mineral, and timber lands. Land reclamation and our national parks are also under its jurisdiction. The following bureaus and services are within this department:

- Bureau of Indian Affairs
- Bureau of Indian Education
- Bureau of Land Management
- Bureau of Ocean Energy Management

- Bureau of Reclamation
- Bureau of Safety and Environmental Enforcement
- National Park Service
- Office of Surface Mining Reclamation and Enforcement
- U.S. Fish and Wildlife Service
- U.S. Geological Survey

The Department of Agriculture develops and executes policy on farming and food. It is concerned with agricultural exports (as well as shipping surplus food to developing countries), food safety, hunger, natural resources (especially our forests and farmlands), and nutrition. They are also responsible for foodstuffs, so they are cognizant of farmland where crops are grown. It provides food to low-income and homeless people throughout the United States. The Department takes the lead in programs to develop communities in rural America.[4] This department also controls our national forests and has many botanists and arborists on its payroll. Quite a few offices are located within Agriculture:

- Agricultural Marketing Service
- Agricultural Research Service
- Animal and Plant Health Inspection Service
- Center for Nutrition Policy and Promotion
- Economic Research Service
- Farm Service Agency
- Food and Nutrition Service
- Food Safety and Inspection Service
- Foreign Agricultural Service
- Forest Service
- National Agricultural Library
- National Agricultural Statistics Service
- National Institute of Food and Agriculture
- Natural Resources Conservation Service
- Risk Management Agency
- Rural Development
- Rural Utilities Service
- Rural Housing Service
- Rural Business-Cooperative Service

---

4. So why does the Department of Agriculture oversee farmland and forests instead of the Department of the Interior? In a word, trees. Because Agriculture has the botanists and plant knowledge, they get custody of the forests. Interior has the geologists and mineralogists, so they have responsibility for the land and minerals.

The Department of Commerce promotes economic development and technological innovation within U.S. industry. It covers such diverse subjects as demographic and economic data, enforcing international trade agreements, the environment, patents and trademarks, and telecommunications. It handles environmental and safety issues pertaining to our atmosphere and oceans, ranging from fish to weather.[5] The fishing industry is largely concerned with sea-based fish such as cod and shellfish and tuna, so because it is a business, it falls under the Commerce umbrella. This department is also responsible for industrial and technological standards. The following activities are located within this department:

- Bureau of Economic Analysis
- Bureau of Industry and Security
- U.S. Census Bureau
- Economic Development Administration
- International Trade Administration
- Minority Business Development Agency
- National Institute of Standards and Technology
- National Oceanic and Atmospheric Administration
- National Technical Information Service
- National Telecommunications and Information Administration
- U.S. Patent and Trademark Office

The Department of Labor promotes the welfare of the labor force and retirees. It handles such responsibilities as collective bargaining, employment discrimination, job training, minimum hourly and overtime pay, retirement and health care benefits, safe working conditions, and unemployment insurance. It also conducts numerous quantitative collections and statistical analyses in employment and price levels. Labor includes the following offices:

- Bureau of International Labor Affairs
- Bureau of Labor Statistics
- Centers for Faith and Opportunity Initiatives
- Employee Benefits Security Administration
- Employees' Compensation Appeals Board
- Employment and Training Administration
- Mine Safety and Health Administration
- Occupational Safety and Health Administration
- Office of Federal Contract Compliance Programs

---

5. The Department of the Interior is responsible for game fish in our lakes and streams since there is limited commercial application and those waters lie within our national boundaries.

- Office of Labor-Management Standards
- Office of Workers' Compensation Programs
- Pension Benefit Guaranty Corporation
- Veterans' Employment and Training Service
- Wage and Hour Division
- Women's Bureau

The Department of Health and Human Services focuses on disease outbreaks and prevention, food and drug safety, health and social science research, and health coverage. It also includes nurse home visitation and Head Start programs. It contains programs for community and faith-based activities, Native Americans, and senior citizens. Both Medicare and Medicaid are handled through this department. This scope requires numerous activities:

- Administration for Children and Families
- Administration for Community Living
- Agency for Healthcare Research and Quality
- Agency for Toxic Substances and Disease Registry
- Center for Faith-Based and Neighborhood Partnerships
- Centers for Disease Control and Prevention
- Centers for Medicare & Medicaid Services
- Departmental Appeals Board
- Food and Drug Administration
- Health Resources and Services Administration
- Indian Health Service
- National Institutes of Health
- Office for Civil Rights
- Office of Global Affairs
- Office of Intergovernmental and External Affairs
- Office of Medicare Hearings and Appeals
- Office of the National Coordinator for Health Information Technology
- Substance Abuse and Mental Health Services Administration

The Department of Housing and Urban Development is geared toward developing and improving our communities. It enforces fair housing laws for public and Native American housing. Its mortgage insurance and rent subsidy programs encourage home ownership for families of modest incomes. This is a rather focused department, containing the following entities:

- Center for Faith-based and Neighborhood Partnerships
- Government National Mortgage Association
- Healthy Homes and Lead Hazard Control

- National Fair Housing Training Academy
- Real Estate Assessment Center

The Department of Transportation oversees the efficiency and safety of our roads, rails, maritime, and airways. This mandate also includes commercial motor carriers and hazardous material transport. The following administrations lie within this mandate:

- Federal Aviation Administration
- Federal Highway Administration
- Federal Motor Carrier Safety Administration
- Federal Railroad Administration
- Federal Transit Administration
- Maritime Administration
- National Highway Traffic Safety Administration
- Pipeline and Hazardous Materials Safety Administration
- Saint Lawrence Seaway Development Corporation

The Department of Energy funds scientific research into clean and reliable energy through several laboratories and operational sites. This department investigates genomics and radioactive waste disposal; in fact, it is the largest sponsor of research into the world of physics within the federal government. It also manages nuclear weapons production and security: the Nuclear Regulatory Agency (which is now part of the Department of Energy) was charged with oversight of all nuclear programs in this nation. This includes private and state-run nuclear power plants as well as reactors onboard naval ships. (The Navy does work hand-in-hand with Energy on matters relating to our shipboard reactors, but Energy remains in charge of the reactor program.) This department contains the following administrations:

- Advanced Research Projects Agency—Energy
- Bonneville Power Administration
- Federal Energy Regulatory Commission
- National Laboratory Operations Board
- National Nuclear Security Administration
- Office of Artificial Intelligence and Technology
- Office of Technology Transitions
- Southeastern Power Administration
- Southwestern Power Administration
- U.S. Energy Information Administration
- Western Area Power Administration

The Department of Education promotes access to and excellence in educational opportunities. Its largest program concerns financial aid for college. It also ensures civil rights and equal opportunity in our nation's school systems and institutions. This is another focused department, which includes the following offices:

- The Institute of Education Sciences
- The Office of English Language Acquisition, Language Enhancement and Academic Achievement for Limited English Proficient Students
- The Office of Elementary and Secondary Education
- The Office of Innovation and Improvement
- The Office of Postsecondary Education
- The Office of Safe and Drug-Free Schools
- The Office of Special Education and Rehabilitative Services
- The Office of Federal Student Aid
- The Office of Vocational and Adult Education

The Department of Veterans Affairs administers benefit programs for veterans and their families and survivors (roughly 70 million people in total). These benefits include burial, compensation, disability, education, home loans, life insurance, medical care, pension, survivor, and vocational rehabilitation benefits. It also maintains cemeteries and medical centers. Medical centers serving veterans have received criticism in recent years for delays in providing healthcare to veterans and for sloppy scheduling and bookkeeping. Yet another focused department, it includes three administrations:

- National Cemetery Administration
- Veterans Benefits Administration
- Veterans Health Administrations

The Department of Homeland Security is the latest addition (2002) to the cabinet-level departments, but is already larger than all but two. It is intended to prevent and disrupt terrorist attacks, protect our critical infrastructure and resources, and collect and share intelligence to respond to and recover from such incidents. It also protects our borders and foreign dignitaries (including the president and those in line of succession) and responds to natural disasters. This department has a broad scope of responsibilities, including the following agencies:

- Countering Weapons of Mass Destruction Office
- Cybersecurity and Infrastructure Security Agency
- Federal Emergency Management Agency

- Federal Law Enforcement Training Center
- Transportation Security Administration
- U.S. Citizenship and Immigration Services
- U.S. Coast Guard
- U.S. Customs and Border Protection
- U.S. Immigration and Customs Enforcement
- U.S. Secret Service

There are dozens of *independent government agencies* which are not part of any cabinet-level department. Independent agencies are established at the request of Congress to be watchdogs of specific sectors of the economy. They must therefore remain independent of the cabinet departments, even though they also report to the president. If there is a difference of opinion or turf battle between departments or agencies, the president settles the dispute. These agencies each have their own charter and mission, ranging from intelligence gathering to consumer protection to space exploration to delivering the mail. These include:[6]

- Advisory Council on Historic Preservation
- American Battle Monuments Commission
- Board of Governors of the Federal Reserve System
- Broadcasting Board of Governors
- Central Intelligence Agency
- Commodity Futures Trading Commission
- Consumer Financial Protection Bureau
- Consumer Product Safety Commission
- Corporation for National & Community Service
- Environmental Protection Agency
- Equal Employment Opportunity Commission
- Farm Credit Administration
- Federal Communications Commission (FCC)
- Federal Deposit Insurance Corporation (FDIC)
- Federal Election Commission
- Federal Energy Regulatory Commission
- Federal Housing Finance Agency
- Federal Labor Relations Authority
- Federal Laboratory Consortium for Technology Transfer
- Federal Maritime Commission
- Federal Mine Safety and Health Review Commission
- Federal Retirement Thrift Investment Board

---

6. Library of Congress, "Official US Government Executive Web Sites."

- Federal Trade Commission
- General Services Administration
- Institute of Museum and Library Services
- International Boundary & Water Commission
- Merit Systems Protection Board
- National Aeronautics and Space Administration (NASA)
- National Archives and Records Administration
- National Capital Planning Commission
- National Council on Disability
- National Credit Union Administration
- National Endowment for the Arts
- National Endowment for the Humanities
- National Indian Gaming Commission
- National Labor Relations Board
- National Mediation Board
- National Railroad Passenger Corporation (AMTRAK)
- National Science Foundation
- National Transportation Safety Board
- Nuclear Regulatory Commission
- Nuclear Waste Technical Review Board
- Occupational Safety and Health Review Commission
- Office of Government Ethics
- Office of Personnel Management
- Overseas Private Investment Corporation
- Peace Corps
- Pension Benefit Guaranty Corporation
- Postal Regulatory Commission
- Railroad Retirement Board
- Securities and Exchange Commission (SEC)
- Selective Service System
- Small Business Administration
- Smithsonian Institution
- Social Security Administration
- Tennessee Valley Authority
- Thrift Savings Plan
- United States Agency for International Development
- United States International Trade Commission
- United States Postal Service
- United States Trade and Development Agency

Some of these agencies are quite interesting and warrant further comment. The Central Intelligence Agency (CIA) uses human source collection and other means to gather, correlate, evaluate, and disseminate national security intelligence. It also directs and coordinates intelligence collecting outside the United States by various elements. However, it does not carry out internal security functions nor exercise any law enforcement power.

The Equal Employment Opportunity Commission enforces laws prohibiting employment discrimination of prescribed factors, including complaints by civil servants against their federal employer. The Farm Credit Administration ensures the safe and sound operation of the banks, associations, and service organizations who loan to farmers, and protects the interests of the borrowers from system institutions and their securities investments. The Federal Communications Commission regulates interstate and foreign communications by cable, radio, satellite, television, and wire. The Federal Deposit Insurance Corporation preserves and promotes public confidence in U.S. financial institutions by insuring bank and thrift deposits, examining state-chartered banks, and liquidating assets of failed institutions.

The General Services Administration (GSA) handles acquisition, real estate, and technology services for the government. They are responsible for office and space management, communications, and transportation for most non-DoD federal facilities. They manage or rent a lot of office space (more than 1,500 buildings, which I am told equates to about 370 million square feet) and a huge fleet (more than 200,000) of vehicles for government use. GSA operations impact every agency and department in the government in terms of office operations and space management.

The National Aeronautics and Space Administration (NASA) advances aeronautic research, explores space, and pursues related scientific discoveries, with several research centers scattered across the country. It is definitely one of the most attractive agencies in the federal government—what child hasn't wondered what is out there and marveled at the wonders of our solar system and outer space? NASA has fallen on hard times in recent years due to budget cuts. However, a recent initiative by President Trump to revisit the Moon and Mars could reenergize this agency.

The National Archives and Records Administration preserves the records of the U.S. government, so that the American public can use and learn from our documentary heritage. To ensure proper documentation of the government's activities and policies, this agency develops standards and guidelines to manage its recorded information. It also approves disposition schedules, agency records, and management practices and stores inactive records.

The Securities and Exchange Commission protects investors, facilitates capital formation, and maintains efficient and orderly markets by reviewing disclosure statements of securities issuers and regulating investment advisors, mutual funds, and securities markets. The Small Business Administration assists and advises entrepreneurs to protect their business interests and preserves free and competitive enterprise. It has a loan program for small businesses and has programs to promote federal contracting to firms run by members of designated socioeconomic groups.

The Smithsonian Institution increases the wealth of human knowledge through 19 museums, a zoo, and nine research facilities. It is a favorite tourist destination in Washington, D.C. (It took me three months of weekends to see it all—at least the public sites in the tour book!)

The Social Security Administration manages the disability, retirement, and survivors' insurance programs that provide Supplemental Security Income for the aged, blind, and disabled. It also assigns Social Security numbers to U.S. citizens and maintains earnings records based on those numbers. This is the largest social welfare program in the country, comprising roughly 20 percent of the total federal budget.

The United States Postal Service provides universal mail service of more than 150 million articles a year with over half-a-million employees. It is unusual within the federal government in that it is run on a for-profit basis. However, it has not achieved this goal for several years and must therefore receive congressional permission to raise its rates. Although some people may call for privatization of mail delivery, I have never seen much support on Capitol Hill for such a move. Instead, I have heard fears that local post offices will close and leave citizens without a convenient place to conduct their postal business. Such fears have persuaded Congress members and vocal constituents to reject privatization.

As you can see, there are a plethora of interest areas available within the federal government. Pursue those agencies which interest you. Hence, my first lesson of government work:

* * *

Lesson #1: Share the mission and values of the agency.

* * *

It does neither the applicant nor the agency any good if there are no shared values. If you do not believe in a strong national defense, you should not consider working for the Department of Defense or an intelligence agency for employment. Similarly, all the employees I have ever encountered in the Department of the Interior are deeply committed to preserving our history or natural resources. If this is something of interest to you, then by all means consider applying. But if you could not care less about history or natural resources or wildlife, then take a pass and consider going elsewhere. Similar aspects of deep interest apply to other departments and agencies listed above. So follow your heart in your job search.

Chapter 3

The Civil Service

In the early years of our government, all positions in the executive branch were filled at the pleasure of the president. As a result, political allies were hired based on patronage to those who paid political parties with their effort and money, regardless of their merit to perform the job. Recalling the old adage "To the victor goes the spoils," this was known as the *spoils system*. Incompetence and indifference ran throughout the government, unless an issue came up of great importance to the president or his party in Congress, in which case it went to the front of the line and all else stopped. Once a president left office, his successor was free to fire anybody he chose and replace him with his own political cronies.

Obviously, this methodology regularly led to waste, abuse, and incompetence. Then in 1881, an event occurred that galvanized opposition to this mindset. President James A. Garfield was assassinated by a man (Charles Guiteau) who was upset that Garfield had not installed him into a political position he thought was owed to him. Garfield's successor, Chester Arthur, had been an official in New York City who had experienced first-hand the reforms that city enjoyed when hiring based on merit rather than patronage. This spirit was enacted into law in 1883 with the Civil Service Act, commonly known as the Pendleton Act after a critical sponsor, Senator George Pendleton of Ohio.[1]

The Pendleton Act provided for a number of reforms to clean up the mess in the civil service. It established a Civil Service Commission of three members to supervise the program. A series of grades was established to provide higher pay rates for more difficult work and for managers. All hires were subject to a probationary period, typically one year, which is why new hires

---

1. 22 Stat. 403, Office of the Federal Register, *United States Statutes at Large.*

are deemed *career-conditional* upon hire. The law struck at the spoils system by forbidding any obligation by the employee to support a political fund or service, as well as any coercion by managers for a political objective.

The law also required all applicants to take a civil service examination consisting of multiple-choice questions to assess their aptitude for working within the federal government. This exam (and yes, I took it as a condition for my job application) was somewhat like the aptitude tests every teenager takes who wants to enter a four-year college. However, during the 1970s there was criticism that such a test discriminated against applicants who came from poor backgrounds and therefore were deprived of the same educational opportunities that other applicants enjoyed. Hence, the exam was abolished and not replaced. (The foreign service and some law enforcement positions still require written exams, however.)

Also during the 1970s occurred our withdrawal from Vietnam, the Watergate scandal, and a public loss of confidence in government leaders. These upheavals led to the Civil Service Reform Act of 1978.[2] This law prohibited discrimination in employment based on marital status or political activity or affiliation. It also created the Merit Systems Protection Board to enforce these anti-discriminatory provisions. The law also created the Federal Labor Relations Authority to protect federal employees who create or join a labor union to enter into a collective bargaining agreement with their department or agency.

Yet another agency was created as a result of the Reform Act. The *Office of Personnel Management* (*OPM*) is an independent agency that is responsible for human resources issues across the federal government, principally administrative law and retirement. It provides guidance and advice to the various departments and agencies on employment issues such as appointments, promotions, reinstatements, temporary appointments, transfers, veterans' preference, and workforce planning. OPM directs and sets policy for affirmative action programs for the disabled, minorities, and veterans within the federal government. These programs address recruiting, retention, training, and promotion of these individuals. It gathers multitudes of data and generates reports on how each department and agency performs in these regards. OPM also manages numerous activities that directly affect the well-being of the federal employee and indirectly enhance employee effectiveness.

In 2015, OPM was subject to a major data breach impacting more than 21 million persons.[3] The data included addresses, fingerprints, and Social Security numbers. The breach was allegedly conducted by agents in China.

---

2. 5 U.S.C. 11.
3. Zengerle and Cassella, "Estimate of Americans Hit by Government Personnel Data Hack Skyrockets," Reuters.

To date, no evidence of an actual release of the information has been found. A report by the GAO recommended 80 specific remediation actions, most of which have been implemented by OPM.[4]

TYPES OF SERVICES IN THE CIVIL SERVICE

There are actually three different services within the federal civil service:

- competitive,
- excepted, and
- Senior Executive.

The *competitive service* is the one we think of most often. It contains positions which are filled on a traditional, competitive basis by assessing the merits of each candidate, conducting interviews, and selecting the best person. Once in the competitive service, employees who successfully complete their probationary period (varying by agency between one and three years) enjoy virtually guaranteed employment. It is very difficult to fire a career employee—the individual must first receive a negative annual performance appraisal, then a 30-day notice, written reasons for dismissal, and a formal hearing (all with the assistance of private legal counsel) before dismissal can occur.

I worked once with a civil servant who did get fired; in fact, he was my office roommate. He was a nice guy with many years of experience but was totally incapable of meeting a deadline. He always turned even the simplest task into a monumental project of excessively complicated paperwork and consequent time wasting. He was impervious to management directives to complete any task because he was convinced that his way of revising everything was the right way, the only way. This process of dismissal took two years and goodness-knows how many man-hours of work. So yes, it happens, people do get fired, but it is painful for all parties (including the taxpayers).

By contrast, the *excepted service* is used to fill intelligence and security positions by considering other factors, such as suitability and lifestyle for such sensitive assignments. Though still competitive in their hiring approach, this process is highlighted by different hiring practices and evaluation criteria unique to the department or agency. These employees may have a two-year probationary period, less often one year. They can be dismissed instantly for certain reasons such as security violations or illegal drug use; however, dismissal for poor performance is still difficult to achieve. The excepted service includes:

---

4. Marks, "OPM Is Still Far Behind on Data Protection Three Years after Devastating Breach," Nextgov.

- attorneys for many departments and agencies,
- Central Intelligence Agency,
- Defense Intelligence Agency,
- Environmental Protection Agency laboratory researchers and related managers,
- Federal Aviation Administration air marshals,
- Federal Bureau of Investigation,
- Foreign Service within the Department of State,
- intelligence offices within DoD,
- most employees within the legislative branch,
- National Security Agency,
- patent examiners,
- Presidential Fellows,
- Public Health Service scientists, clinicians, researchers, and related managers,
- Secret Service, and
- teachers within the DoD Dependent Schools.

These agencies contend that they need greater speed and flexibility to fill vacancies than is available through normal hiring channels, plus they need to eliminate some employment protections available to the excepted service. For example, these agencies usually subject their employees to random drug testing and will not provide a "safe haven" to drug users, as would be available in the competitive service.

Most excepted service positions fall under one of four schedules, lettered A through D. Schedule A covers positions which are not conducive to examination. Subject professions include attorneys, chaplains, and physicians, as well as disabled persons and positions in remote and hard-to-access locations. Schedule B positions are not susceptible to a competitive examination but must nonetheless meet specified qualification standards for the position. These positions are professional, scientific, or technical in nature. Schedule C appointments are of a political nature to a position that is either confidential to a cabinet-level official or else in a policy-making role. Schedule D positions cover fellowships and interns.

As the third type of employment service, the *Senior Executive Service* covers leadership positions on a noncompetitive basis, and includes both jobs based on merit as well as those filled for political purposes. They are not of cabinet rank, and 90 percent of them are career appointments (not more than 10 percent are political appointees). However, they are all senior managers or policy makers throughout departments and agencies, serving above the pay grades of the General Schedule.

Note that in all three types of service, federal civil servants do not have the right to strike. Striking is prohibited by law.[5] They do have the right to collective bargaining but cannot negotiate

- employee benefits,
- job classification,
- pay rates,
- picketing that disrupts operations (though informational picketing is allowed),
- right to strike or other concerted action, and
- total hours worked.

Clearly, there are several types of alternatives to the common competitive service. These alternatives have limitations in terms of permanency, drug use, security clearance, and so forth. The applicant must consider these restrictions and decide if they are acceptable to career plans and lifestyle.

* * *

Lesson #2: Observe the limitations of the service for which you apply.

* * *

Schedule B positions especially come under this rule because they often involve classified work or specialized scientific or technical work. If your lifestyle is not conducive to obtaining and maintaining a security clearance, then you should consider another avenue to federal employment. Similarly, if you do not embrace the political and policy goals of the current administration, then Schedule C is not an option for you.

GENERAL SCHEDULE GRADE SERIES

Several different salary tables exist for federal positions.[6] Regardless of which service one is considering, most federal jobs are based on the General Schedule (GS) grade series. It contains 15 grades of increasing responsibility and salary. GS-1 is reserved for individuals who have no high school diploma and limited skills as well as high school student-interns and involves unskilled labor activities such as carrying boxes around a warehouse or to a

---

5. 5 U.S.C. 7101 et al.
6. They are all listed at www.opm.gov/policy-data-oversight/pay-leave/salaries-wages/#url=2019.

loading dock.[7] Grades increase based on educational background, so GS-2 is geared to high school graduates with no college, GS-3 is reserved for those with only one year of college or work experience, and GS-4 is used for those with two years of college (such as an associate's degree) or work experience. GS-5 applies to those with a bachelor's degree, so many new hires straight out of college begin at this grade level. GS-7 is reserved for those with one year of graduate school or professional work experience, GS-9 for people holding a master's or law degree (or two years of professional experience), and GS-11 for a doctorate or advanced law degree (or three years of professional experience). This means that many new hires out of college spend one year as a GS-5, a second year at the GS-7 grade, and at least a third year as a GS-9.

Notice that the above covers only odd-numbered grades. Many of the GS-2 through 4 positions are secretarial in nature because they enlist people who do not have bachelor's degrees. GS-6, 8, and 10 are reserved for clerical personnel such as office assistants and storekeepers. The exact grade depends on the amount of managerial work involved or how high your boss ranks. Many of these positions do not require a college degree.

GS-11 through 15 is where the bulk of office professionals will be found. Again, the exact grade depends on the work to be done, as well as how much supervision the individual requires from higher management. The higher the grade, the more complex the work and the greater the years of experience required to perform. In fact, many first-line managerial positions are within this grade range.

Alternatively, the federal government also maintains a Wage Grade (WG) series for employees paid by the hour, largely blue-collar workers. These are principally craft and trade professions. Additionally, special rate tables exist for certain agencies for certain labor categories (such as administrative law judges and law enforcement officers) and the Senior Executive Service.

There are also summer internships available for students attending school at least half-time, both high school–level and college-level. These young people can gain valuable experience and perhaps course credit for their work. Individual agencies and departments announce these vacancies every October, and they fill up quickly due to their popularity.

All grades have a series of ten steps with successively higher pay rates to cover cost-of-living increases.[8] Even if an employee does not receive a promotion in a given year, a step increase may be in the offing. For the first three years in grade, an employee receives a step increase yearly. For steps 4 through 6, the step increase occurs every other year. For steps 7 through 9,

---

7. Crosby, "How to Get a Job in the Federal Government," *Occupational Outlook Quarterly*.
8. There is an exception to the ten-step arrangement which I will discuss later.

the increase is every three years. Upon reaching step 10, the employee is now receiving the maximum allowable pay for that grade.

The pay rates for all schedules are set by regulation from OPM and are not subject to negotiation by the applicant or employee. However, certain high-cost areas (approximately 50, give or take) have pay differentials (known as *locality pay*) which increase the salary levels by a predetermined percentage for that area. For instance, I was once offered a job in San Diego which offered a pay raise of 1.5 percent over the same grade in Washington, D.C., due to the higher cost of living in southern California.

All these pay rate tables can be adjusted annually based on whether Congress has granted a cost of living adjustment. This is totally a political decision reached during congressional deliberations on the budget and is by no means guaranteed. This is the only way an employee in step 10 for a given pay grade can ever get a pay raise without first obtaining a promotion.

BENEFITS

There are many fringe benefits available to federal employees. Everybody gets paid on a biweekly basis, usually every other Thursday. With a 52-week calendar year, this means 26 paychecks per year. Civil servants get used to two paychecks per month very easily. With twelve calendar months, this means that an employee will expect to receive a third monthly check twice a year. Quite a cause for celebration!

Each employee earns 13 days of sick leave per year, or four hours per period. This leave accumulates forever but is subject to challenge by management if it is concerned that the employee is abusing the privilege. Any employee who uses more than three consecutive days of sick leave will probably be asked to bring a doctor's note to verify their condition or illness.

Annual leave is a function of time served. During the first three years of employment, this personal leave accrues based on 13 days per year, again four hours per pay period. Between three and 15 years of service, this rate increases to 6 hours per pay period (with a bonus 4 hours added in the last pay period of the year to make the number of hours work out to an even 20 days). All employees beyond 15 years of service earn 8 hours per pay period, or 26 days per year. However, an employee cannot carry more than 30 days (240 hours) of leave over into the succeeding calendar year—the unused balance is forfeit. This is known as *use-or-lose* and is cause for much planning by federal employees to ensure that no leave is lost.

Annual leave does not suffer the same proof as sick leave, so any employee can ask for annual leave without stating a purpose. Obviously, this privilege is not absolute and can be denied by management if the employee's absence impairs the office mission.

*   *   *

Lesson #3: Plan your use of annual leave judiciously and in advance.

*   *   *

Timing is everything when it comes to scheduling annual leave. Accounting and procurement personnel know not to take leave in September, the end of the fiscal year, which is their busiest time. I once worked with the Federal Emergency Management Agency (FEMA), which is in a reactive mode during the spring mountain runoff due to river flooding, and during the summer and fall due to hurricanes. Once December rolls around and the hurricanes are gone, so are the civil servants—it is not unusual for them to take two or three weeks off during the holidays because their annual leave has piled up so much use-or-lose time. Their offices become very quiet and empty that month!

Federal employees receive ten paid holidays per year. The office is closed and no work is required of most employees, but all continue to receive pay. As is the case with both annual and sick leave, the employee is paid for time off. For this reason, the federal work-year equates to 2,087 hours, which is far more than in the private sector. It is also why hourly rates are higher in the private sector, where there are fewer hours to spread across the salary dollars.

Many offices (though certainly not all) compensate employees for overtime or weekend work. The pay rate is capped at the highest GS-10 step's hourly rate at time-and-a-half, so employees at GS-10 and below receive overtime pay at a rate which is 50 percent higher than their basic pay. Those employees who are GS-11 and higher will be subject to this pay rate cap and, though still compensated for the additional hours, they will not necessarily receive 50 percent more than normal.

Court leave and military leave are common and do not count against the employee's annual or sick leave balances, although employees on jury duty must turn in their court reimbursement checks to avoid suspension of pay. Excused absence is sometimes granted to employees due to hurricanes, snowstorms, or other unexpected tragedies or acts of nature.

Employees are evaluated annually (usually in the late spring or summer) for performance over the past year and are given standards to meet for the next twelve months. These standards are in writing and signed by both employee and supervisor. The evaluation meeting is an opportunity for employee and manager to discuss on-the-job performance and establish methods to improve over the next year. The wise employee will prepare for this meeting by creating discussion points to justify that the past year's performance meets and even exceeds all performance standards.

* * *

Lesson #4: Practice your verbal justification for fulfilling your standards.

* * *

A bonus pool is established for each office and performance bonuses are paid out of the pool. Spot bonuses may also be issued during the year for a particular action taken by an employee. A bonus is by no means guaranteed and is often not of a significant amount to make a big difference in the employee's bank account. However, these performance appraisals are certainly taken into consideration when promotions are offered.

Telecommuting, Flex Time, Work Weeks

Telecommuting or telework is in vogue today to improve employee morale. This entails working from home or a nearby building (such as your favorite corner coffee shop) to contact your workplace computer by using your own laptop or smartphone, while enjoying your favorite latte or herbal tea. This saves nonproductive driving time, takes cars off the highway to limit our carbon footprint, and reduces commuting angst (such as fender-benders and "that lane-changer in front of me"). Agencies benefit by reducing office space and associated lighting costs and dedicated telephone lines.

In 2017, the last year for which OPM has collected and analyzed data, about 43 percent of federal employees were eligible to telecommute.[9] Over the same period however, telecommuting participation was just 21 percent of all employees and 48 percent of those employees who were eligible. Situational telecommuting due to inclement weather and commuting obstructions are the most common form of telework participation. Washington, D.C., is known for becoming paralyzed if only one inch of snow falls, since road clearing downtown is problematic at best, and an ice storm can create absolute paranoia in the local driving public. On these days, civil servants work from home.

According to OPM's statistical analysis of questionnaire results, among those employees who telecommute:[10]

- 83 percent said telework improved their morale,
- 77 percent said telework helped them to better manage stress,

---

9. Office of Personnel Management, "Status of Telework in the Federal Government."
10. Office of Personnel Management, "Status of Telework in the Federal Government," 32.

- 68 percent said telework improved their health,
- 72 percent said telework improved their performance, and
- 64 percent said they telework because it helps maximize their productivity.

Half of the telecommuters work remotely once or twice a week, and another third do so more than twice a week. The rest only telecommute once a month or less.

Note that telecommuting is not an absolute right for the federal employee. The office must first provide such an opportunity and is not mandated to do so if it can argue that physical presence in the office is essential. Actions being taken these days to identify and eliminate artificial barriers to telework include updated policy and guidance, training for managers and employees, upgrading office computer networks to improve remote access, and improved data automation and tracking. But implementation across the federal government remains sporadic at best, often because management cannot or chooses not to implement a telework program. Naturally, jobs which require continuous access to classified material will not be candidates for telework, since the data must stay within the classified spaces of the office.

Telework opportunities vary greatly between agencies. General Services Administration is perhaps the leader in providing telework opportunities for its employees. I have worked in a couple places elsewhere where I only needed to go to the office when meetings were held, not more than twice per week. A friend who worked for the Patent and Trademark Office worked full-time from home, required only to go into the office for one hour each month. On the other hand, some offices will not allow any telework because the employees must attend meetings throughout the day or handle sensitive information. I once worked in an office where I was able (after several attempts) to get approval for telework, but could only do so once because my job required multiple face-to-face meetings every day.

Flexible work schedules are another family-friendly workplace initiative which has had some success (but by no means universal) in the federal government. Some flexible work plans permit either a ten-hour workday four days per week, with the employee taking off every Monday or Friday.[11] Some places (though not many) allow the employee to go home after booking 40 hours (commonly known as *first 40*). I once worked with one ambitious, hardworking employee from such an office who would go home for lunch on Thursday and not come back into the office until the following Monday. Of course, he had no life the first half of the week, but sure had a blast the second half!

---

11. Because the flexible day for shortened work hours is either a Monday or Friday, these are referred to as *sandwich days* because they surround the three midweek days when everyone reports to the office.

Another, more popular approach is a nine-hour workday four days per week. The fifth day (again either Monday or Friday), the employee works a traditional eight hours one week and takes off that day the other week. This allows for an 80-hour pay period, although each week will alternate between 36 and 44 hours. I was able to follow this last method for several years and really enjoyed that long weekend every other week!

All federal offices in the Washington, D.C., area and certain other areas offer a transit subsidy to encourage employees to use public transportation to and from work. The employee receives a pretax stipend (currently capped at $260 per month). For those employees who do not live near public transit, or who operate vanpools, some offices will subsidize their monthly parking fees.

Family-Friendly Programs and Other Benefits

There are family-friendly programs available at some offices. They may offer family leave, especially for a newborn baby. Hence, maternity and paternity leave may be allowed at a given office. Some offices have their own child-care centers on-site or may offer discounted membership to a fitness club. Some have a leave-sharing program, where individuals can contribute up to a week of their own leave into a leave-hours bank for those who face long-term medical absence.

Some offices may offer a relocation bonus to encourage employees to move to a remote or undesirable location, or even a recruitment bonus for attracting new hires. Hazardous duty or environment pay, premium pay, and retention bonuses are sometimes used at certain offices engaged in dangerous work or locations.

The federal government operates a Public Service Loan Forgiveness Program.[12] If the individual has participated in the William D. Ford Federal Direct Loan program for student loans, and has made timely payments every month for ten years (120 months) as a full-time public employee, the balance of the loan may be forgiven.

HEALTH BENEFITS

The federal government offers three types of health programs for employees to opt into. First, the Federal Employee Health Benefits program includes a variety of medical plans, both preferred-provider and defined-benefit types, at benefit levels that generally exceed anything available in the private sector.[13]

12. https://godefense.cpms.osd.mil/loan_forgiveness.aspx.
13. www.opm.gov/healthcare-insurance/healthcare.

There are currently six different fee-for-service carriers licensed nationwide, and many more on a regional or statewide basis. Premiums are withheld from gross pay with pre-tax dollars, so they are not subject to income tax. OPM does not offer, but does not prohibit participation in, pharmacy incentive programs or pharmaceutical co-pay programs. However, Medicare and Medicaid recipients are prohibited from participation in such programs.

Second, the Federal Flexible Spending Account Program allows employees to spend a user-defined amount of dollars for healthcare, usually saving both cash outlay and tax liability without paying a premium.[14] Third, the Federal Employees Dental and Vision Insurance Program specializes in dental and eye care expenses that are not covered by a health plan. Again, all premiums are paid through pre-tax dollars.

For any of these health plans, the employee may elect to include coverage of spouses (at additional cost) and any dependent children under age 26. However, children in same-sex partnerships are not currently covered. Coverage is available to any intermittent, part-time, or temporary employee who works at least 130 hours per month for at least three consecutive months.

There are no waiting periods, no medical examinations, and no restrictions on pre-existing conditions. All plans offer certain free preventative services from a Preferred Provider (e.g., childhood immunizations, screenings for cancer, diabetes and high blood pressure, and tobacco cessation medications). The government pays roughly 70 percent of the premiums, while the employee pays about 30 percent through payroll deduction as pretax dollars, plus any deductible and uncovered expenses for medical service. Enrollment is available during the first 60 days of employment, or after a major life event such as birth, death, or marriage.

Each year from mid-November through mid-December, civil servants have the option of changing their plan to another of the many plans offered by OFPP. This process is known as *open season*. Each plan produces an information brochure which is available free to civil servants through their human resources office.[15] The employee need not take any action if (s)he chooses to remain enrolled with the current plans. Retiring civil servants must have been continuously enrolled for the previous five years to port their enrollment into retirement, otherwise these benefits are not available to retirees.

A retiring employee retains health insurance into retirement at the same rates as current employees—there is no added premium for age or existing condition. Once the employee dies, a surviving spouse may continue coverage for 18 months until selecting another plan outside the government.

---

14. Currently, the employee can carry over $500 of unspent dollars to the next year; any remaining balance is lost.

15. Further information for the current year is available at www.opm.gov/openseason.

OPM has a long-term care program for those employees and retirees who need help with daily activities or who suffer from cognitive disorders.[16] This would cover such tragedies as Alzheimer's or Parkinson's disease, auto or sports accident, multiple sclerosis, old age, or stroke. It covers living at an assisted facility or nursing home as well as the person's normal residence. Any employee who is eligible for the health care program (whether or not actually enrolled) is eligible for this program, as well as all retirees. Current spouses of eligible enrollees are themselves eligible for long-term care, as are adult children and stepchildren, and (for current employees only) parents and in-laws. A physical examination is not required, though a health questionnaire must be answered and acceptance is not guaranteed. Premiums may change over time.

The Federal Employees Group Life Insurance program, the largest group life insurance program in the world, allows a new employee to become covered immediately for a basic level of coverage unless the employee waives coverage.[17] This coverage covers annual salary (rounded up to the next thousand) plus $2,000. Options exist for higher coverage at various multiples of salary, although the cost for these options does increase with age. The government pays two-thirds of the premium and the employee pays one-third. Unlike health insurance, however, premiums are not paid with pre-tax dollars. Additional coverage for a spouse or dependent child under age 22 is also available. This plan should be carefully compared with private plans, since premiums and coverage may vary greatly.

* * *

Lesson #5: Take advantage of the benefits programs available at your office.

* * *

Travel

Travel is a function of the specific position and agency. Some offices have no travel budget and therefore everyone works a traditional workweek at their desks, every week of the year. Other offices require their people to travel during the course of the year, depending on their particular duties. And many offices have infrequent travel occasions.

Once a travel need is identified, the employee fills out a travel request with itinerary plans, and the Travel or Human Resources office will take care of airline reservations and calculate a travel advance payment to cover projected

---

16. www.opm.gov/healthcare-insurance/long-term-care. An alternative source of life insurance is Worldwide Assurance for Employees of Public Agencies (WAEPA).

17. www.opm.gov/healthcare-insurance/life-insurance.

lodging and meals (known as *per diem*). The per diem payment is based on predetermined daily rates for different metropolitan areas of the country. Air travel is arranged by the travel office, since airfares are negotiated by GSA with certain airlines for certain routes. The traveler must personally make hotel and car rental reservations. The traveler must then physically pick up the travel orders, airline reservation details, and per diem check before leaving, since many hotel chains and auto companies negotiate discounted rates with the federal government and will honor them once the traveler arrives with a copy of travel orders in hand.

Upon return to the office, the traveler files a claim to report all expenses and obtain any additional funds owed by the government. Some offices also require the traveler to file a trip report outlining what work was accomplished during the journey.

Charitable Giving

Until the 1950s, federal employee donations to charity were unorganized. Charities were continuously making pleas to office employees throughout the year. Managers would lean on employees to contribute, sometimes against their will. Some people would merely empty their pockets of loose change, with no sense of budgeting or planning. Receipts for tax deductions were unheard of. It was a jumbled mess and quite unpleasant for everyone.

The process began to change in the mid-1950s when some charities combined their fund-raising efforts. However, fund-raising efforts still recurred periodically throughout the year and amounts donated were modest. In the 1960s combined campaigns in certain cities began, where all charities were merged into one major fund-raising drive. This was also the beginning of using payroll deductions to provide donation dollars, hence tax-deduction records. The Combined Federal Campaign has now grown to encompass over 20,000 charities.[18] A massive fund-raising drive is held each autumn during which employees may enroll, change their beneficiary, or withdraw. New hires can enroll upon beginning employment, regardless of the season.

INFORMATION TECHNOLOGY

The federal government probably produces, collects, and distributes more information than any other American entity.[19] Because of the import and

---

18. www.opm.gov/combined-federal-campaign.
19. Lindner, 179–81.

scope of these information activities, the management of federal information resources is a critical issue for its employees. Each agency must consider:

- accommodations for individuals with disabilities;
- emergency preparedness;
- energy efficiency;
- environmental assessment of hardware;
- evolving information technology through market research and refreshment;
- national security;
- protection of privacy; and
- security of resources.

The federal government makes extensive use of *information systems* which process data, facts (often not for public release), and opinions, for a number of processes (e.g., audiovisual presentations, cartography, payment data, and reports).

Under the Information Technology Management Reform Act, the Department of Commerce issues standards and guidelines for federal computer systems to ensure security and interoperability.[20] Known as the *Federal Information Processing Standards (FIPS)*, they are approved by the Secretary of Commerce and issued by the National Institute of Standards and Technology (NIST).[21] NIST is the organization which develops and maintains publications for national standards and measurements. These standards and guidelines are issued as FIPS for use government-wide and as industry standards to promote interoperability and security.

FIPS are compulsory and binding for federal agencies and contractors, which cannot waive their use. NIST has also issued a series of Special Publications which are gaining increasing utility throughout the federal government as de facto standards for information system security, as well as usage in the academic and corporate sectors. These standards provide technical controls to protect the confidentiality, integrity, and availability of stored data, and prescribe automated procedures to analyze and remediate vulnerabilities and weaknesses. Those who manage information systems must therefore:

- control connections to external information systems;
- control information posted or processed on publicly accessible or web-based information systems;

---

20. 40 U.S.C. 25.
21. FIPS standards are located at www.nist.gov/itl/itl-publications/federal-information-processing-standards-fips.

- identify and authenticate identities of devices, processes, or users requesting access;
- identify, report, and correct information and system flaws;
- limit physical access to authorized information equipment, systems, and their operating environments;
- maintain subnetworks for publicly accessible system components so that they are logically or physically separated from internal networks;
- monitor and protect communications at the system's external boundaries and key internal boundaries;
- monitor visitor activity and maintain audit logs of physical access;
- periodically scan the system and files from external sources as applications are downloaded or executed;
- protect the system from malicious code and update mechanisms when new releases are available; and
- sanitize or destroy media before disposal or reuse.

*   *   *

Lesson #6: Limit your computer operations to work-related tasks.

*   *   *

Every user in a federal office is subject to constant monitoring. So are the websites you visit. Therefore, keep your Internet usage to work-related sites and refrain from controversial and social websites during work hours. Similarly, compose your shopping list on your home computer, not the one at work. Work is also not the place to download or upload your vacation photos or play funny cat videos. You can be cited for improper usage and be disciplined, or even fired.

In accordance with section 508 of the Rehabilitation Act of 1973, federal employees and citizens with disabilities must be able to access and use data to the same extent as their colleagues without disabilities.[22] However, these requirements do not apply to a:

- national security system;[23]
- project or effort incidental to a contract;
- repair or occasional monitoring of equipment; or
- situation which would impose an undue difficulty or expense on the agency.

---

22. 29 U.S.C. 794d. See also Department of Energy, "Architectural and Transportation Barriers Compliance Board Electronic and Information Technology (EIT) Accessibility Standards (36 CFR 1194)."

23. The functions of such a system involve intelligence and cryptologic activities, command and control of military forces, integral components of a weapon system, or fulfillment of military or intelligence missions. This definition does not include routine administrative and business applications (e.g., finance, logistics, payroll, and personnel management).

Concerns over software vulnerabilities and malicious code, and the risks they introduce to information systems, have promoted the concept of *software assurance*. This approach provides a level of confidence that the software operates as intended and is free from defects. Pioneered by the Departments of Defense and Homeland Security, a working group developed guidance on how to include software assurance considerations in the acquisition process and build security into the software.[24] This has now become a paramount concern in software development and operations to mitigate risk. This guidance is also intended to minimize harm that may result from the loss, misuse, or unauthorized access to (or modification of) the system itself or the information it manages.

Networked computers exchange information by cable or wireless connection between data links.[25] As such, several aspects of networking become important to keep in mind. *Network architecture* is a framework to specify an information system's physical components and their configuration, data formats, and operating principles and procedures. A telecommunications network architecture may also include a description of products and services delivered, and detailed rate and billing structures. Network architecture often includes the classification and structure of a distributed application architecture. This means that one's desktop or laptop computer in the office may be "talking" to a server in another state, or maybe just down the hallway. Many government agencies have moved to centralized servers to reduce overhead expenses, so distributed computing is pretty much the norm these days in the federal government.

Network monitoring looks for slow or failing components and notifies the network administrator in case of outages. While an intrusion detection system monitors a network for threats from the outside, a network monitoring system looks internally for problems caused by overloaded and/or crashed servers or network connections. Commonly measured metrics in the network monitoring process are response time and availability. If a connection cannot be re-established or times out, or a document or message cannot be retrieved, the monitoring system sends an alarm e-mail to the administrator. An automatic failover system may be activated to remove the troubled server from operation.

All information systems require qualified people to serve as network administrators to monitor their performance, respond to security incidents, and update systems. These services may be performed in-house or contracted out, since they are commercial in nature. These administrators patch software with

---

24. Detailed guidance is found in Polydys and Wisseman, "Software Assurance in Acquisition." This document is managed by the United States Computer Emergency Readiness Team within the Department of Homeland Security.
25. Lindner, 183–84.

the latest upgrades, usually overnight and on weekends to minimize work disruption. They also report any suspicious activity, both on the network and via unauthorized access from outside.

A major part of a network administrator's job is setting up and repairing accounts through a help desk. Each user is given a username based on a standard syntax which may vary with each office, and guidelines for selecting a password. The user is responsible for creating, remembering, and protecting this password. Since half of all calls to a help desk involve compromised or forgotten passwords, it is essential that the user remember it.

*　*　*

Lesson #7: Remember and protect your password.

*　*　*

Commit your password to memory. Remember it like you remember your family members' names. Don't write it on a sticky note and paste it on your computer—that is a security violation (and looks dumb). A favorite trick of hackers is to call up and pretend to be with the help desk, then ask for your password. The real help desk doesn't care what your password is—if you forget it, they will erase it and enable you to create a new one while masking your keystrokes so they don't see it on their monitors. Hence, don't give your password to anyone—ever.

Some offices provide employees with a laptop which they can take on official travel and maybe home. This permits them to work remotely from home and telework. The agency will usually require the employee to connect directly to the office server via virtual private network to avoid eavesdropping by external parties.

Chapter 4

How to Get a Job

As you can see, each of these departments and agencies has their own mission, and their employees are dedicated to that mission. So to begin your job search, assess your values and decide where a good fit would be.

*   *   *

Lesson #8: Take stock of yourself and your strengths—and what you want to do.

*   *   *

Applying for a federal job is similar yet different from a private sector application.[1] Both the federal and private sectors look for proper experience and accomplishments. But the federal government requires more information from its applicants, may require a much longer resume (three to six pages rather than just one), uses occupational questionnaires, overtly incorporates socioeconomic preferences, and posts most job opportunities in one central location. And the federal government does not as a rule bother to check references (an exception is within the intelligence community). The search and application process is free—no need to hire a search firm or pay a website. The steps for applying for a federal job are outlined below.

THE JOB POSTING AND APPLICATIONS

First, the applicant must establish an account on USAJOBS: www.usajobs .com. All positions in the executive branch competitive service are listed as *vacancy announcements*, which could exceed 10,000 on any given day. It

---

1. An excellent source of information for federal job seekers is https://gogovernment.org.

does not include positions in the judicial or legislative branches, excepted service, or short-term positions lasting less than six months (for these, you must go to the specific agency's website for information). An account with USAJOBS allows you to

- complete a personal profile that includes citizenship and contact information,
- search for positions of interest (both automatically and manually by answering queries),
- double-check that you qualify,
- filter openings by agency or location or salary,
- save as many as ten searches of interest,
- develop a resume or upload an already-prepared resume (up to five per account) and any other prepared document file (such as cover letters, proof of eligibility for government employment on a Standard Form 50, college transcripts, and military service to obtain veterans preference), and
- apply for a position and track status of same.[2]

Veterans transitioning out of the military are a common source of talent for new civil servants. They already work in the federal government and have bought into its mission and standards. Plus, the government fully endorses the "Hire the Vet" concept. The website www.military.com has an app to download for Google Play or iTunes for military who wish to transition to civil service.[3]

Each vacancy announcement contains a job title, agency, location, salary range, and (importantly) announcement number. You will need to refer to this number when following up on any application, so record it in a safe file when you apply. The job title not only defines the job content, it also reflects a four-digit number that identifies the grade series (usually either GS or WG) of the position.

*   *   *

Lesson #9: Keep a file record of every job you have applied for.

*   *   *

I have come across several job titles which differ from any counterpart in the private sector. A *program analyst* assesses how well a specific program is performing in terms of meeting objectives and consuming resources (money, talent, and time). A *budget analyst* focuses on the money aspect of

---

2. The online resume builder replaces the Optional Form 612, which is now obsolete.
3. www.military.com/military-transition/employment-and-career-planning/work-for-the-dod .html.

performance. A *management analyst* looks at specific agency or department performance, rather than a specific program. Also, a *technical writer* in the private sector is limited to an engineering or scientific realm, but in the federal government it can also relate to computer operations or legal affairs.

The salary is usually a range where an entry-level individual will start at the bottom of the range and a more experienced civil servant will be at a different point in the range, based upon the number of years of experience. The position may have promotion potential up to a higher grade, which can be filled based on length of time and performance. The announcement will also contain a due date, when applications must be received by the close of business; latecomers will not be considered.

* * *

Lesson #10: Apply immediately—don't risk missing the application deadline.

* * *

When applying to a job posting, all required documents are due at the same time—and a missing document will kill your application. Some announcements may say "open until filled" or "Open Announcement," in which case the agency is either posting a hard-to-fill position or else has a number of positions of the same type to fill (often entry-level) and wants to collect multiple applicants for ongoing and future needs. Some jobs are reserved for current or former federal employees, veterans, or disabled people who meet specific conditions. These vacancy announcements will say something like "Status candidates only" and specify the limitation. Jobs open to the public will say something like "Open to all qualified candidates" or "Open to all U.S. citizens." Often, this section is called *Area of Consideration*.

Note that the job location is listed. Despite the popular conception about centralization, about 85 percent of all federal jobs are located *outside* the Washington, D.C., metropolitan area. They are spread among all 50 states and six territories or commonwealths, as well as at foreign installations and embassies. So, a candidate with geographic preferences and restrictions must pay heed to job location. You can query the USAJOBS database geographically to help in this search.

Each announcement states whether the position is full-time (most are), part-time, seasonal, or temporary. Most career positions are conditional for a period of three years, during which the employee is under probation to demonstrate basic competency and justification for earning public trust. Temporary positions are never more than two years in duration, usually less.

The announcement will then discuss the position itself regarding the agency mission, key requirements, and any required travel. Job duties are spelled out, often in a bulleted list, but in fairly great depth. One of the requirements will say *other duties as assigned*, which is a catchall phrase for doing things that are not on the list but need to be done in the office (anything from mentoring a new employee to hanging ornaments for the office Christmas party). Then comes the qualifications needed for the position in terms of education, work experience, and any specialized skills.

* * *

Lesson #11: Make sure you meet *every* requirement for the position.

* * *

You must be qualified in all criteria for requirements—coming close or fulfilling "all but one" will not get you anything but a rejection. Job criteria are not subject to negotiation. Make sure you have the necessary college degree, professional certifications, and security clearance, no matter how extensive your experience, since these are often "gates" that each applicant must pass through before receiving any consideration for an interview.

Other items of interest that may be included could be payment of relocation expenses (increasingly rare in the federal government) and any accommodations for those with physical disabilities. Any requirement to furnish references will also be specified, but this is unusual. Any security clearance requirements will also be announced.

The announcement often has a "How to Apply" section that identifies any supporting documents you must upload to complete your application. This is intended to determine eligibility for the job and could include anything from a college transcript to the proverbial questionnaire about your career accomplishments.

Veteran's preference may also be allowed by the agency for those who served at least 180 days in the armed forces and received an honorable discharge. As a rule of thumb, for two candidates who are similarly qualified for a given position, status as a veteran enhances your chances of hire by about 10 percent. Sometimes a wounded veteran or Purple Heart recipient will get even more of a preference. Likewise, volunteers from the Peace Corps or AmeriCorps (VISTA) will receive credit for one year of federal service. Military spouses and disabled citizens may also receive preferential treatment from a specific agency.

Many applications require the applicant to complete a questionnaire developed by the agency. Applying online can populate some background information already entered by the applicant, but specific multiple-choice or true-false questions need to be answered for each individual announcement by the applicant because they are tailored to the individual position. This questionnaire is not the same as your Scholastic Aptitude Test—instead, the questions explore your experiential *Knowledge, Skills, and Abilities (KSAs)* about the specific job duties reflected in the announcement.[4]

Many questionnaires also contain a brief essay to provide specific examples of how your work experience fulfills the job duties, including outcomes and compliance with federal regulations and guidelines. This is your chance to show off your expertise, since the federal government prides itself on hiring experts. These statements are typically 200 to 400 words in length. They are usually written in paragraph format but can be a bulleted list. Be succinct and get to the point from the start. Proofread to eliminate all grammatical and factual mistakes, and make sure your writing style is consistent across all documents to avoid sending a "cut-and-paste" message, which will surely be picked up by the evaluators.

*   *   *

Lesson #12: List specific examples of your accomplishments.

*   *   *

RESUMES

Tailoring your resume to the particular job is desirable because you can then emphasize the keywords used in the announcement and show the agency that you put time and effort into the application. But more important is to tailor your cover letter to reflect the keywords and highlight the experiences and skills the agency most covets.

In your resume, list and discuss the jobs you've held in reverse chronological order, beginning with your current position and working backwards to your first relevant job. Frequent job changes must be explained, as they give the impression that either you cannot hold a job or are easily frustrated or impatient on the job. You can expect to summarize each older job in about 200 words and more recent and relevant ones in about 400 words. Focus on examples of accomplishments, especially if they can be quantified. And keep repeating the keywords you find in the announcement, since agencies tend to computer-scan applications and count points every time they spot a keyword use.

Your resume must list all education levels, from high school through college and graduate school to work-related courses. Some offices require the

---

4. Other nomenclature used include "desired qualifications," "ranking factors," "selective factors," or "evaluation methods." They all mean the same thing: the skills the agency is looking for in their new hire.

applicant to submit a grade-point average. If so, they will generally consider a floor average, such as 3.0, to be necessary to fulfill the duties of the job. They do not officially consider a university or college's reputation, so a 3.1 average at an obscure state university counts more than a 2.9 from Harvard. This may not seem fair to a student who proudly sought and studied at a more prestigious school, but the government really has no basis to hire based on college reputation.

Your related skills should over any computer programs with which you are proficient. Most federal offices use Microsoft applications, so Word and Excel are a must for all, and PowerPoint and Project are essential for many.

* * *

Lesson #13: Become proficient with Microsoft Office.

* * *

If you feel that you are rusty or only have basic skills, consider taking a course. The time won't be wasted.

Don't forget professional licenses and certificates, foreign language proficiencies (including sign language), and performance awards. In fact, many offices now require certifications as "gatekeeper" mechanisms: certifications and awards and such don't necessarily help you get the job, but they will eliminate those applicants who aren't certified.

And don't forget to spellcheck all documents.

* * *

Lesson #14: Update your resumé frequently.

* * *

Since you never know when a job opportunity will arise, it is necessary to keep your resume current. Add every change in duties, every new training course, and every performance appraisal or award as they occur. These updates will save hours later when you may have limited time to respond to a vacancy announcement. It will also give you a conscious pat-on-the-back for your latest accomplishment!

INTERVIEWING

The hiring agency will review all applications to identify who is qualified. Those who are not qualified receive no further consideration and will be so notified. Applications which are qualified will next be submitted to a review panel of professionals in the career field, who will review the applications in detail and rank them by the criteria set forth in the vacancy announcement. Those applicants who are the most highly qualified (at least three) will be referred to the office with the vacancy, where the managers will conduct interviews and select their preferred choice.

Interviews may be done over the phone or in person, at the agency's discretion. Phone interviews have the advantages of saving you travel time and allowing you to take notes, but you won't be able to see the office personnel for physical reactions (unless you are on Skype). In a phone interview, then, you will have to consider tone of voice (both yours and theirs) when addressing a question. If possible, use a landline to eliminate static and clarify all communications. I once met a manager who would angrily hang up any phone call once he learned that the other person was using a cell phone—he would not accept their callbacks, either. To avoid offending the interviewer and ensure a clear channel of communication, use a landline.

In-person interviews require more preparation.[5] Research the agency thoroughly beforehand and be familiar with its mission. Practice questions and answers before you leave in a mock interview, especially guessing what questions they might ask you, and prepare your answers by feeding back the keywords in the vacancy announcement. If you must have a cup of coffee before the meeting, don't spill it on your clothing. Make sure your hair is combed, necktie straight, shoes shined, and clothing and makeup in order. And get a good night's sleep. Note that the resume is the only reading matter you should have in your possession—leave the newspaper at home. Have extra copies of your resume with you.

If you're traveling to a place you have never have been to, you must have directions. You might consider going through a dry run to visit the interview location beforehand to account for traffic delays and unknown territory. Most smartphones are already loaded with a GPS navigation system, but make sure you have it handy.

*   *   *

Lesson #15: Do a practice interview.

*   *   *

At one point in my career when I was looking for a promotion and a change of scenery, I applied for an interesting position, was selected for an interview, and then thoroughly bombed out! I had not interviewed for more than five years and the rust showed. I then applied for a job at an office where I had no real interest in working but where I knew that my resume would be of

---

5. Vilorio, "Working for the Federal Government: Part 2," Bureau of Labor Statistics.

interest. Sure enough, I was selected for an interview and used the occasion to sharpen my interview skills. I actually did get a job offer and had to go through the process of turning them down. But it set me up for a successful interview on my next application, which did result in a job offer and four years in a good position.

The interview may be conducted by one person or a panel of several people. There may be multiple rounds of interviews—this is not common at many agencies, but will certainly occur in the intelligence world. The first interview will focus on prepared questions specifically related to the job, so forget about the "puffed-up questions" that job search books pose (like "What is your favorite television show and why?"). All interviewees will receive the same questions to ensure fairness and establish a common baseline for all the competing applicants. This means that government interviews tend to be more formal than in the private sector—nobody will offer you a cup of coffee or a chance to relax, and you will be herded out of the office like a dog as soon as it is over.

Answer each question after a moment of reflection. Don't ramble. Don't show arrogance, no matter how important you think your position is. Be ready with your own questions that are related to the job such as office mission, overtime, schedule flexibility, or telework. Do try to remember the names of the interviewers. These first interviews tend to run for 30 to 45 minutes. When this first interview concludes, remember to say thank-you with a follow-up e-mail to show genuine interest in the job.

Follow-up interviews determine whether a well-qualified candidate will be a good fit within the office and agency mission. They tend to be conducted on-site. This is a great time to see the office and how people dress—to see if you will fit in. A follow-up interview is not common outside the intelligence world, so an invitation to one means you are a leading candidate (or even "the" candidate).

When the interviewing panel makes a selection, they will send the results to Human Resources, who will verify such personnel issues as security clearance and make a formal job offer. The applicant must direct a response to Human Resources (not the employing office) because only they have the authority to hire. All unsuccessful applicants receive a pro forma notice indicating whether they were qualified and referred, or else rejected as not qualified and a reason why.

For a current federal employee changing offices, the Human Resources office of the new office must coordinate with their counterpart office supporting where the employee currently works to obtain a release from his/ her current employer. Normally the starting date is at least two full weeks away, although if the position is at the same grade as the applicant currently holds (called a *lateral move*), the current office can hold the individual for 30 days before release.

I do not recommend calling the Human Resources office to determine status of your application. They can only provide canned answers like "your application is in review" or "I haven't heard back yet." There is nothing you can do to hurry up the process. If another office has offered you a job, first, congratulations, and second, you will have to decide if want to work there with no other options in front of you. Remember, you can always say "no, thanks." I did that once, when an interview resulted in a job offer with an agency I decided I did not want to work in. I had applied for a position in another office I really wanted, but they had not even conducted interviews yet. I said no, gambling that my first choice would soon interview me and I would charm them with my experience and good looks. Well, something like that actually did happen and I landed my choice job (though I was told it was only because of my experience). My gamble did pay off.

INTERNSHIPS

For college students, internships are available within the Executive Office of the President for 90-day periods, consistent with college semester and summer schedules. These positions do not pay a salary; applicants are motivated by the experience and possible college course credit. Individual agencies have their own internships, many of which do pay a salary. A student will have to conduct research into each agency or use their college job search office to learn about these opportunities.

THE FEDERAL JOB FORCE AND YOUTH

Unfortunately, the federal government has a real problem attracting young people under age 30. OPM reports that only 127,000 permanent employees are under 30 years of age, whereas 274,000 are over 60.[6] Based on a permanent workforce of just over 2 million people, that means roughly 6 percent are just starting their careers, yet nearly 14 percent are looking at retirement in the near future. Recent college graduates are often excluding federal employment from their career aspirations because they want a different type of work environment. As a result, only about 28 percent of all new hires are under 30. Even worse, student internships are further limited to just 15 percent of

---

6. Neal, "Government Hiring Young People Continues to Be Terrible."

all those students who obtained full-time employment last year for a given department or agency. If an agency did not convince at least seven student interns to join up full-time last year, it cannot hire any students at all this year.

These problems are not new; I have heard about them for years. However, it is getting worse every year. A much-feared "retirement tsunami" will occur some day when these older employees finally decide to call it quits. Civil servants in this age zone continue to work to build up pension and social security payments and wait for an "early-out" retirement bonus, as well as love of the job. If these bonuses ever become common, or civil servants get frustrated at work due to lack of pay raises or new punitive regulations, they will leave in droves. This issue is much discussed among older civilian employees at the office water cooler. I cannot count how many times I have heard older workers say, "I'm just waiting for an early-out." They could leave at any time, but don't. But if they do, the federal government will have a real problem filling its positions.

GRADE CREEP

All federal jobs are classified at a specific grade based upon job content. OPM issues guidance for the local human resource office to review and classify by grade every federal position. Entry-level positions below a journeyman level may be filled at a lower level by a trainee, who then works over time to develop the skills and experience necessary to achieve fully successful performance at the designated grade. For such an individual, this becomes a *target grade* to achieve over time. This process is based on the Classification Act of 1949, established at a time in postwar America when most civil servants were GS-5 or lower, without a college degree, and primarily clerical in work duties.

My, how times have changed! Today there are 2.1 million civil servants, of which 2 million are professional rather than clerical in nature, often with college degrees. Only 0.1 million are still clerical in nature, roughly 5 percent of the work force.[7] The loss of clerical positions is due to changing times, automation, or outsourcing. This introduces a new problem into the federal workforce—*grade creep.*

This problem is most prominently displayed in the nation's capital, where perhaps one third of all employees are graded GS-14 or -15, and another third are GS-12 and -13. The primary cause of this issue is competition for the labor market from outside sources—the commercial sector, local government, or nonprofit organizations. I have personally seen this problem occur at one

---

7. Neal, "Where Have All the Classifiers Gone?"

agency which has found it necessary to offer promotions to outside individuals to lure them onto the payroll. Sadly, this office has a reputation for heavy turnover, as these people come onboard for the promotion, then leave eight months later to work elsewhere at the same grade.

Occasionally, the human resources office will conduct a *desk audit* to verify that a particular job is properly graded. I have seen two instances where a GS-14 underwent an audit and was shocked to learn that their duties actually justified a grade 15. The government was then bound to offer the incumbent a non-competitive promotion on the spot. I had worked closely with one of these persons for years. He was a dedicated engineer who unfortunately spoke his mind frequently, earning the disapproval of upper management and a series of denials for competitive promotions. He must have been ecstatic when he heard the news that he was getting a promotion after all!

The process of job classification itself has become something of a lost art, since human resources specialists focus on other areas of concern these days, such as affirmative action and hiring new employees. This means that the requiring office develops the job requirements, with an eye toward emphasizing higher-end skills to increase the grade level. Accurate job descriptions are not necessarily paramount anymore: a 2016 study reported a 30 percent inaccuracy figure. Advice from Human Resources may not be forthcoming due to their lack of experience in classification skills. Hence, the problem of grade creep will continue for the foreseeable future.

LAYOFFS AND THE STOPPER LIST

Layoffs are uncommon but not unheard of within the federal government. Whenever a budget cut or change in responsibilities dictates a reduction in staffing level, a layoff may be necessary. This is known in bureaucratese as a *reduction of force*, or *RIF*. There are specific procedures to be followed by all parties to ensure fairness and alleviate this condition as quickly as possible.

The department or agency will immediately freeze all hiring from the outside. The scope of the freeze is determined by the administrator of the organization. All affected persons go onto a *stopper list*, which is mandatory for consideration for any open positions. The human resources office reviews the resume of each affected person and identifies all job categories for which (s)he is qualified. Persons on the list have little input into this process.

Should an office within the organization wish to fill an affected position, it must restrict consideration to those names on the stopper list. The human resources office will send three names on the list to the office with the opening, which must then select one of them for the position. Interviews are recommended but not always required, especially if the office knows one of the persons from prior employment or experience. Anybody who is interviewed and not selected is returned to the list without penalty to be considered for another position.

If the position is located within the same commuting area at the same grade, the person must accept the position or else lose government employment. If the position is one grade below the current grade, the individual must still accept the position or else lose employment. If the position is two grades below the current grade, the individual is free to turn it down and retain a spot on the stopper list without penalty. If the position is more than two grades down, then human resources might still offer the position but not expect acceptance, and the individual again maintains enrollment on the stopper list.

Note that the human resources office makes no attempt at ensuring a fit between enrollee and acquiring office. Their goal is to remove all names from the stopper list as quickly as possible. Elimination of the list permits resumption of normal procedures for vacancy announcements and outside hiring. This process often takes months to complete.

Operational offices universally hate this process. They cannot recruit and attract talent from outside sources while handicapped with a stopper list. And they may be forced to accept someone from the stopper list they don't really want. As a result, many offices will suspend announcing vacancies until the list is depleted, in hopes that some other office will take ownership of the problem.

Chapter 5

Retirement

The *Civil Service Retirement System* (*CSRS*) was created in 1920 to provide civil servants with benefits for retirement, disability, and survivorship. This system provides a defined-benefit pension-type plan without Social Security participation or any sort of retirement savings plan. It was superseded in 1987 for new hires with another system so that anybody hired subsequently was no longer enrolled in it. However, current retirees (and some long-term employees) are still drawing benefits from CSRS.

The new system from 1987 is the *Federal Employees Retirement System* (*FERS*), which remains in use today. All incoming employees participate in this new system, but employees hired before 1987 had the choice of transitioning over or else remaining under CSRS. This means that those civil servants who chose to convert are covered by two retirement systems. FERS contains all three types of benefit plans: retirement, Social Security, and savings. The employee pays into both the retirement and Social Security funds in a defined amount through a payroll deduction, while the federal government matches this amount.[1] The savings plan is discretionary with a chosen level of participation by the employee, again with matching funds. Retirees then receive monthly annuity payments for the rest of their lives, with survivor benefits.

Note that CSRS did not pay into Social Security, hence retirees with only CSRS benefits do not accrue social security quarters or payout. Those retirees with both CSRS and FERS benefits will only accrue social security benefits for the time when they were covered under FERS.

---

1. The Social Security component for federal retirees under FERS is the same as for the private sector, so it will not be examined here. For further information, see the Social Security Administration website at www.ssa.gov.

TYPES OF RETIREMENT

There are five different types of retirement in the federal government:

- voluntary,
- involuntary,
- disability,
- early, and
- deferred.

Critical to this discussion of lifetime benefits is the definition of *retirement*. Eligibility for retirement is based on a combination of age and years served. The "minimum retirement age" is prescribed in a sliding scale based on year of birth. For those born in or after the year 1970, the minimum age is 57, whereas for those born in earlier years the minimum age is reduced on a sliding scale. For those born in or before 1948, the minimum age is 55. A minimum of 30 years of service is required to obtain full benefits. If the individual of retirement age chooses to retire with fewer than 30 years, the retirement benefit is reduced by five percent for each year of service below 30. Simple arithmetic tells us that someone with less than 10 years of experience would receive no retirement benefit at all, since the five-percent rule would erode any payout.

However, there are quite a few circumstances which would allow retirement with immediate benefits. If the individual is 60 years old with 20 years of service, or 62 years old with just five years of experience, (s)he can *voluntarily* retire and begin drawing benefits within 30 days. Of course, the level of benefits will be adjusted based on the actual length of service, but retirement is nonetheless recognized.

An individual who has not served 30 years (or 20 years if already age 60), but has served at least ten years, may nonetheless choose to retire from the civil service for personal reasons. As with other early retirees, his/her benefit will be reduced at an annualized rate of 5 percent for each year below age 62. If this person chooses to hold off taking the benefit until reaching age 62, then this 5 percent setoff will disappear.

Another possible situation occurs when an individual *involuntarily* retires early due to circumstances beyond his/her control, such as a job elimination. This individual must be either 50 years old with 20 years of experience, or else any age with 25 years of service. So if a position in Washington, D.C., is abolished due to budget cuts and the employee is offered a position on the West Coast, say, immediate retirement is possible with either combination of years and service. The five percent setoff provision also applies to anybody who does not have the right combination of age and years yet faces involuntary retirement due to reduction-in-force or relocation of function outside the local commuting range, provided (s)he has at least ten years of federal work experience.[2]

Disability retirement is possible for anybody with a mere 18 months of service due to long-term (at least one year) disease or injury, provided the agency has unsuccessfully tried to reassign the individual at the same grade level in the same commuting area.

Occasionally, a particular agency will decide to motivate older workers to retire. This usually occurs if it needs to reduce staffing due to budget reductions. It will offer to pay a lump sum to anyone who accepts. This lump sum is known as an *early-out* bonus. I have known many older civil servants of retirement age who stay on the job, saying "I'm just waiting to see what they do about early-outs." These offers are so uncommon that these people usually have to retire on a different schedule, sadly in many cases when their health is in jeopardy or they just get tired of working.

An agency might offer early-out to reduce its payroll, since older workers tend to be on the upper end of the pay scale. This avoids layoffs, since these older workers would merely *bump-out* younger workers who might be more effective in current and future working conditions. Of course, there could be other, more nefarious reasons for office management to decide on this course of action. Any early-out decision must be approved by OPM.

Finally, any employee with five years of service can leave the government and later choose to draw *deferred* retirement benefits upon reaching age 62, even if enjoying a career in the private sector.

THE FINANCIALS

*   *   *

Lesson #16: Consider a retirement date in your financial planning.

*   *   *

As for determining the amount of the monthly payment for any retiree, a calculation is made by identifying the three-year period in which the individual earned his/her highest salary level. For most people, this will be their final three years of service. This is referred to as a *high-three* average salary. This

---

2. This benefit for involuntary retirement does not apply if the individual is offered another position within the commuting range at the same grade or not more than two grades lower.

calculation includes pay raises and shift differentials but does not include any overtime or bonuses. Every year, some partisans call to increase this calculation to a high-five average, which could drive down one's retirement pay due to including lower-paid years in the calculation. However, this initiative has not yet succeeded in passing Congress.

This high-three amount will be measured at one percent for each year of service. Unused sick leave is added to years of service for this purpose. So if someone retires at age 60 with 20 years of service, (s)he will earn one percent of salary per year of service. If (s)he retires at 62 with only 17 years of service, (s)he will also earn one percent per year. But if the individual retires at age 62 with 20 years of service, (s)he will earn 1.1 percent of salary per year.[3] Those persons who were in the CSRS before enrolling in FERS will get an additional benefit based on the CSRS enrollment (1.5 percent for the first five years within CSRS, 1.75 percent for the next five years and 2 percent for all successive years). Higher rates apply for certain law enforcement officers, air traffic controllers, couriers, and congressional employees and members. Once the employee reaches age 62, (s)he is eligible for cost-of-living increases which are calculated at one percentage point below the Consumer Pricing Index issued annually by the Bureau of Labor Statistics, Department of Labor.

There may also be an annual cost-of-living increase granted by Congress. This is the one aspect of retirement which is at the mercy of Congress, since motions are submitted every year to reduce this adjustment in order to save money. All other efforts to change retirement payout calculations tend to be defeated by a significant lobbying effort by civil servants, both current and retired, who do not hesitate to remind representatives that they vote by their pocketbooks.

One need not be employed continuously by the federal government to meet these eligibility requirements. Someone who has the right combination of age and years can leave federal employment for the private sector and become eligible for a deferred annuity on the date on which both criteria apply. Alternatively, they can apply for a lump-sum payout. Or, a civil servant may leave government service and return years later; their retirement calculations pick up where they left off.

Most veterans of the uniformed services cannot credit their term of service to FERS without waiving their military benefits.[4] However, a veteran who is disabled in the line of duty, or who retires from a Reserve component, may be credited with service time without penalty to military pay.

---

3. Higher percentages apply for members of Congress and their employees, as well as certain law enforcement officials, air traffic controllers, firefighters, and nuclear materials carriers.

4. The term "uniformed services" includes active-duty military, reserve military, National Guard, and commissioned members of the Public Health Services.

Disability retirement benefits are the same as for other retirees if the individual is 62 years old or else meets the age-and-years-of-service requirements for immediate retirement. If not, then benefits are calculated at a significant reduction: 60 percent less a total setoff of Social Security benefits for the first year of payout, and 40 percent less 60 percent of the Social Security benefit thereafter. Survivor benefits are also reduced based on a prescribed scale.

Clearly, planning is critical to determining when to retire. Employees begin to think about retirement as early as five years before separation, and actively plan one year before they leave. Seminars are regularly provided for free by Human Resources to help guide the employee who is contemplating retirement. There is also a plethora of free advice offered online by a variety of entities.[5]

The *Thrift Savings Plan* (*TSP*) is one of the most significant benefits of working for the federal government.[6] It is a retirement savings/investment plan for federal employees and military members. Established in 1986, it offers savings and tax benefits comparable to those offered by many private corporations to their employees under 401(k) plans. TSP is a defined contribution plan, such that the retirement income received by a given retiree depends on how the amount invested during his/her working years and the earnings accumulated over that time. The plan is managed by an independent federal agency, the Federal Retirement Thrift Investment Board, whose five directors are appointed by the president. The board's mission is to manage the TSP with financial prudence in the interest of the participants and their beneficiaries without regard to political pressure.

A savings plan has many advantages for the employee. It permits contributions to be allocated before taxable income levels are calculated (hence the term *pre-tax dollars*) to avoid paying income tax on money you won't see until after retirement, at which time all withdrawals are subject to income tax. Of course, the individual will presumably be retired by this time, so his/her income level will not have a salary and therefore be in a lower tax bracket. By contrast, a Roth contribution works in the opposite direction: contributions come out of taxable income but all withdrawals are tax-free, including interest earnings. Administrative expenses are kept low to comply with the spirit in which the program was established. Plans from previous non-federal employers can be rolled into a TSP account. There are also certain circumstances in which an employee can obtain a loan from his/her TSP account or even withdraw a dollar amount while still employed.

---

5. The single most reliable source of information on the Internet is Mike Causey, who writes a daily column for www.federalnewsnetwork.com. Mike has been around Washington forever, it seems, and has accurate and current information on a variety of topics for federal employees and retirees.

6. Its website is www.tsp.gov.

The government automatically creates an account for the employee and contributes an amount equal to 1 percent of salary each pay period, regardless of employee participation. On top of this, the employee can choose to contribute five percent of basic pay, for which the federal government will contribute matching funds. In other words, an employee who chooses to contribute five percent of salary not only escapes income tax on that five percent, but really obtains 11 percent as a contribution level thanks to government participation. The employee can contribute an additional five percent of salary, though without any matching funds from the government. Moreover, once the employee reaches age 50, the five percent ceiling is lifted and a greater amount may be contributed.

*   *   *

Lesson #17: Contribute the maximum amount of money you can (your retired self will thank you).

*   *   *

There are currently six different funds to choose from, all pegged to standard market indices:

- common stocks,
- fixed-income bonds,
- government securities,
- international stocks,
- lifetime funds weighted among the other five funds based on particular age groups, and
- small-cap business stocks.

An employee can withdraw funds from the plan either upon retirement, upon reaching age 70½, or upon retirement if still working at age 70½.[7] The government has just instituted a policy as this book is written which permits partial withdrawals, so the retiree under age 70½ need no longer withdraw the entire amount at once.

Upon death of the employee, an amount equal to one-half the remaining balance may be paid to the surviving spouse. If the employee divorced and did not remarry, then the previous spouse qualifies. If no spouse survives, any dependent child under 18 qualifies for survivor benefits. A child of greater age may still qualify if disabled or a fulltime student.

---

7. Note that the federal government does not have a mandatory retirement age for most employees, only for those who require physical fitness, such as law enforcement officers.

*   *   *

Lesson #18: Leave instructions for your family for after you pass away.

*   *   *

I have a document for my wife and another for my children that goes through all the details of what to do after I pass away. These documents tell them where to go and how to apply for survivorship benefits. Since I won't be here to tell them personally, this is the best way to explain it to them, since none of them works for the federal government or understands its retirement payout policies.

FERS has a death benefit payable to the designated beneficiary equal to one-half of the regular monthly retirement benefit. Of course, if the retiree named multiple beneficiaries, then the monthly payout is equally split between them. If no beneficiary survives, then a widow(er) will receive the payout. A child of the deceased may receive a monthly payout if under 18 (or 22 if a full-time student) or older if unmarried and disabled based on a condition incurred while still a minor.[8] If there is no surviving spouse or child, then a surviving parent(s) will be compensated. Failing that, the executor of the employee's estate receives full payout. If none of the above applies, then the guidelines of the employee's state of residence will be followed to determine who receives the benefit. If no beneficiary can be determined, then the benefit goes into the Civil Service Retirement and Disability Fund.

---

8. There will be an offset equal to that calculated for Social Security purposes which might be so great as to obviate any survivorship benefit.

Chapter 6

Classified Work

The Department of Defense (commonly known as *DoD*) is the largest employer in the United States, with 2.15 million uniformed members of the armed forces and 732,000 civilian employees.[1] Three major departments comprise the DoD: Army, Navy, and Air Force. The Marine Corps is not a separate department—it is part of the Department of the Navy. A number of agencies are also part of the defense department without being a part of any of the services—these are referred to as *purple agencies* because their many differently uniformed members create a mish-mash of colors.

In addition to the three major service departments, numerous other agencies are within the Department of Defense:[2]

- Defense Advanced Research Projects Agency
- Defense Commissary Agency
- Defense Contract Management Agency
- Defense Finance and Accounting Service
- Defense Health Agency
- Defense Information Security Agency
- Defense Intelligence Agency
- Department of Defense Education Activity
- Defense Logistics Agency
- Defense Security Cooperation Agency
- Defense Security Service
- Defense Threat Reduction Agency

---

1. DoD Public Affairs, "Our Story."
2. Defense Acquisition University, *PGI Procedures, Guidance and Information.*

- Joint Improvised Explosive Device Defeat Organization
- Missile Defense Agency
- National Geospatial-Intelligence Agency
- National Security Agency
- United States Special Operations Command
- United States Transportation Command
- Washington Headquarters Services.

Within each military department, the secretary is the person in ultimate charge. These are cabinet-level positions subject to Senate confirmation. Every secretary has a deputy to ensure continuity of service, such as when the secretary is on travel and somebody has to stay home to run the department. In fact, the deputy is often involved in day-to-day activities while the secretary minds the "big picture" expressing the administration's vision in congressional testimony and public appearances throughout the country.

Each department has a plethora of assistant secretaries to handle specific areas of daily activities. These positions vary from one department to another. The one constant is that somebody serves as the comptroller of the department—the person responsible for collecting and disbursing funds—and is usually ranked first among equal assistant secretaries. Another assistant secretary is responsible for acquisition and a third for manpower. The various military departments also have an assistant secretary for installations and environmental concerns.[3] The Office of the Secretary of Defense has the same duties but labels these positions as undersecretaries (whereas most other departments retain the traditional assistant designation), and has additional undersecretaries for policy and intelligence.

Defense work is critical because the safety of our nation is at stake, as well as the very lives of our service members. This is the single greatest difference from working in the private sector or in the civilian agencies. Despite the vagaries of budget wars and government shutdowns, the workload is stable and, at the moment, growing. This means greater job security. Today, the DoD is especially eager to find cybersecurity and data professionals, as well as intelligence specialists.

Yet DoD work is not for everyone, especially for many new college graduates. You may work in a classified area where cellphones are collected at the door and not returned until you leave the office. You may not be able to talk to your friends during the day, unless they work in the same environment. Your office may be colorless and windowless. You may be

---

3. At the time of this writing, President Donald Trump recommended the creation of a United States Space Force, and it later was signed into existence on December 20, 2019, as an independent branch of the armed forces.

up-to-date on current technology, but your boss may not be, which makes you both the smartest person in the office and an associate of those who are not as knowledgeable. An open and collaborative workplace is common at corporate startups and innovative corporations such as Apple and Google, but that is not always the case at defense sites. If you are used to or enjoy an open workplace you may not enjoy the DoD work environment, and therefore might reconsider defense work.

Intelligence is information collected, analyzed, and distributed by agencies to learn what other governments and people are doing, with an eye toward assessing impact on America.[4] Subject areas of concern include foreign hostile governments, narcotics, and terrorism. This entails information which is then submitted to a variety of interested parties such as government agencies (both American and allied), decision-makers, military commanders, and Congress. This also includes counter-intelligence and covert activities to obtain and safeguard this information. These covert activities are conducted overseas without public acknowledgement by the U.S. government to influence media activities or public opinion. This is different from the routine diplomatic mission of the Department of State.

Currently, there are 16 agencies within the Intelligence Community. Within the Department of Defense, we have the Defense Intelligence Agency, National Geospatial-Intelligence Agency, National Reconnaissance Office, and National Security Agency. All four of the armed services are represented (25th Air Force, Army Intelligence and Security Command, Marine Corps Intelligence Command, and Office of Naval Intelligence). The Central Intelligence Agency is of course present. The Department of Justice is well represented by both the Drug Enforcement Agency and the Federal Bureau of Investigation. Department of Homeland Security has its Office of Intelligence and Analysis, as well as the Coast Guard Intelligence office. Three other departments are also represented within the Intelligence Community: Energy, State, and Treasury.

The National Intelligence Program, led by the Director of National Intelligence, includes all intelligence activities where results of the analysis are shared by two or more agencies. This does not include the Military Intelligence Program, which involves information of interest solely to the Department of Defense, primarily to plan and conduct joint tactical operations.

Of course, where these interest areas overlap, turf battles and information sharing become problematic. This became painfully obvious after the terrorist attacks of 9/11, when it was discovered that intelligence which could have alerted us to terrorist activity was not being shared because other agencies'

---

4. Executive Order 12333.

personnel did not have the proper clearances or an individual agency would not give up ownership of the information. Efforts to put the director of the CIA in charge of the intelligence community failed because its director has no say over ongoing operations of other agencies. Hence, Congress passed the Intelligence Reform and Terrorism Prevention Act in 2004 to create a separate office, the Director of National Intelligence (DNI).[5] This individual controls the budget for the entire National Intelligence Program and sets the objectives and priorities for same. This official also is responsible for collecting, analyzing, and disseminating the intelligence gathered by the various agencies listed above. However, DNI still has no authority over specific activities within each agency, nor does (s)he have the ability to hire, fire, or transfer employees of individual agencies. Hence, it is not really correct to assume that we have one "intelligence czar" because turf battles and refusal to share information are still possible and not readily obvious to outside officials (including Congress and the press).

There are several sources of information that are collected by the intelligence community. Signals intelligence (SIGINT) involves information gleaned from signals transmitted either by people or machine. Training courses will explain that there are two other subcategories within SIGINT. One common source is communications intelligence (COMINT), messages between people obtained by eavesdropping and wiretapping. This information is examined to identify the person transmitting, where from, when and how long (and if it is repeated periodically), frequency employed, encryption (as opposed to clear text) and language, and addressees. The other subcategory is electronics intelligence (ELINT), which involves electromagnetic radiations from nuclear explosions or radioactivity, aircraft, radar, and surface-to-air missiles.[6]

Financial intelligence (FININT) collects information about financial transactions to discern their capabilities and motives. This type of intelligence is primarily used by law enforcement agencies to identify money laundering or tax evasion.

Human intelligence (HUMINT) is the sexy and adventurous part of intelligence gathering. This involves interrogating prisoners of war (both our side and theirs), refugees, and travelers. If an individual is detained in a prison, then the guards can also provide information. Debriefings of returning diplomats and military patrol personnel are also beneficial. It also includes clandestine activities by non-military agencies (such as the CIA) doing "James Bond

---

5. 118 Stat. 3638.

6. Some practitioners will argue that ELINT and SIGINT are really subcategories of COMINT. This is an academic argument without any apparent benefit to the reader. I chose to make SIGINT that main category because it seems more logical and clearer to both the author and the reader.

stuff" to gather information. This agency is the subject of many television shows and movies which provide fictional depictions of its daily operations.[7]

Imagery intelligence (IMINT) is gathered by reconnaissance planes and satellites to monitor activity on the ground. Such imagery is collected either by air or in space. Airplanes fly so much closer to the ground that they provide a higher resolution; however, satellites are not vulnerable (yet) to attack and can cover a wider range of the earth's surface.

Measurement and signaling intelligence (MASINT) examines technical characteristics (signatures) of designated technical objects. This would include acoustic and radar signals, biological and chemical sources, and nuclear emissions. It is not a stretch to say that MASINT uses the same techniques as astronomers, who acquire and analyze light, radio, and X-ray emissions from heavenly bodies, except that MASINT is looking toward Earth rather than outer space. It uses sensors (some of which are undoubtedly clandestinely placed) to obtain information on:

- biological and chemical features;
- emissions of electromagnetic, nuclear, and thermal energy;
- magnetic flux and anomalies;
- material composition;
- mechanical sound, such as an engine or propeller;
- motion due to flight or vibration;
- nuclear features; and
- reflected radio frequency, light, and sound.

Clearly, this is the most scientific form of intelligence gathering.

Open source intelligence (OSINT) involves gathering information from publicly acknowledged sources that are often unclassified. This includes:

- commercial literature, financial reports, and databases;
- internet such as blogs, discussion groups, online publications, and social media websites;
- media such as magazines, newspapers, radio, and television;
- professional and academic conferences, journals, papers, and theses; and
- public government data such as budgets, hearings, reports, speeches, telephone directories, and websites.

Ironically, the greatest source of OSINT may well be the Federal Research Division of the Library of Congress, which has a wealth of information available

---

7. Personally, I am partial to the television series *Covert Affairs*, which had some elements of reality in it.

to the general public for a fee. OSINT may help to better understand the context of classified information and fill in gaps in our knowledge.

Finally, we have Technical Intelligence (TECHINT) to analyze weapon systems rather than their signatures to better understand how they are made and work. The intents of this effort are to prompt reverse engineering to develop effective countermeasures and to reproduce systems of interest.

Job tasks in the intelligence community are not much different from the unclassified world. They also include the following unique positions:

- analysts to assess the information,
- case officers to recruit field officers (sometimes called "handlers"),
- collections officers to obtain the intelligence (usually by technical means),
- counterintelligence law enforcement officers to hunt for moles and foreign spies,
- field officers to collect intelligence in foreign countries, and
- operations officers to try to prevent foreign groups or governments from interfering or reacting to our collection efforts.

Otherwise, life is the same as in the rest of the government. Bureaucracy, meetings, and paperwork abound. They dress the same as other civil servants, not like the operatives in the *Men in Black* movies or J. Edgar Hoover's FBI G-men. Come to think of it, dress-down mode is more typical: some of the people I have seen in a couple of these offices look like they just rolled out of bed—and dress like it, too. Sometimes I think that the Woodstock or grunge generations have returned in the form of intelligence analysts!

The biggest difference from the competitive service is that they cannot talk about their work outside the office. Yet they do have a life outside of the office. Two members of the adult volleyball team I coached worked in the CIA. One of the fathers in our Boy Scout troop was an analyst for the CIA and was sent to Saudi Arabia for several months at the onset of Operation Enduring Freedom with only a couple days of notice. That event was actually doubly detrimental to our troop, as our committee chairman had to give up his role because he was reviewing so much data at his day job at NSA that he wasn't getting home until 8:00 at night. Even non-analysts must be cleared, including janitors and maintenance workers. One classified agency I worked at cleared its fitness instructor, just in case he overheard any classified discussion.

*   *   *

Lesson #19: Make sure you and your family are comfortable with working in the military or intelligence areas when considering your career.

*   *   *

The classified and political nature of this world must be acceptable to you and your family members before entering it.[8] I knew a young woman who broke up with her boyfriend, a DoD employee, specifically because she was philosophically opposed to the current level of U.S. defense spending. She may be right or wrong, but clearly she could not accept his career aspirations. I also heard of a man who was turned down for a classified assignment because he and his wife shared everything about their workday, and he would not be able to do so without revealing classified information. This can take a toll on family life, so consider carefully whether your family can adjust to what one of my friends called "The World of Shhh."

The total budget of classified intelligence and military operations is steeped in mystery. One source claims that the current fiscal year budget request is over $81 billion to cover such operations.[9] If the numbers are correct, then the national intelligence budget is roughly $60 billion and the military intelligence budget is around $21 billion per year. These numbers include classified hardware development and production, such as airplanes, satellites, and weapons, as well as intelligence operations. That is a lot of money and it grows every year. Needless to say, there are plenty of job opportunities in this realm for those who are interested and can get cleared.

There are many operations within the federal government which require access to restricted information which should not be released to the general public. These positions employ persons who have a "need to know" certain classified information to do their jobs. Because the people who handle this information must be trusted to protect this information to avoid an adverse effect on national security should it be released, a process has been set up to assure that they are reliable, responsible, and trustworthy. Many military personnel obtain clearances as a requirement for their job, then carry the clearance into their civilian career. Other careers which may require clearances for sensitive positions include education, financial, intelligence, medical, and telecommunications. It is axiomatic that a clearance can add up to $15,000 to one's annual salary, since employers need not pay for the clearance process for someone already cleared, and is certain to obtain a dependable and well-disciplined employee. If roughly 3 million federal employees (both civilian and military) have some level of clearance, then perhaps half as many in the contractor community do.

There are different levels of classification based upon the relative damage that could be caused by their disclosure of this information, which is assessed and established by the agency itself and is not subject to debate by an

8. Continuing a previous point on relevant television shows, I found that *The Unit* provided an excellent depiction of the impact of classified work on family life.

9. Rosenberg, "Trump Administration Asks for $81.1 Billion Black Budget, the Largest Ever," *The Fiscal Times*.

outside party. This means that an applicant who is cleared to a lower level cannot try to negotiate the agency to accept their lower level. Similarly, an applicant who does not desire to be considered for a security clearance will not receive further consideration for that position. The different levels of classification include:

- Unclassified
  - Unclassified/For Official Use Only
  - Controlled/Unclassified
  - Public Trust
- Confidential
- Secret
  - Secret/Sensitive Compartmentalized Information
- Top Secret
  - Top Secret/Sensitive Compartmentalized Information

The lowest level of interest is *Unclassified*, which is information that can be released to the public without fear of damage. Examples include press releases, items of interest to the general public, and reports to disseminate information to advance commercial technology. Sometimes, the fact that a higher-classified program exists could be unclassified.

A variant of this approach is *Unclassified/For Official Use Only*, where dissemination would not harm the national security but nonetheless would be troublesome. A good example of this is an office telephone list. An agency's Office of Public Affairs can release its own telephone list, since they must maintain two-way communications with the public, but would not be authorized to release telephone lists of internal offices.

The next level would be *Controlled/Unclassified*. The concern here is that dissemination of such information is illegal, though not necessarily sensitive to national security. For example, detailed information of the operation of federal office systems (such as a computer network) may be proprietary to the manufacturer and public release may violate a *non-disclosure agreement* (NDA) with the company. Government employees and contractors would sign their own NDA to protect such information but would not necessarily be subject to obtaining a clearance.

Next comes the *Public Trust* designation. Any release of information would present a moderate or high risk of impacting the efficiency and/or integrity of the agency/department mission. The agency/department determines whether the risk is high, moderate, or low. Low risk usually does not require any background investigation, but high or moderate risk does. For example, employees in the Social Security Administration handle my Social Security number routinely; if one of their employees should sell my number to a criminal, (s)he has betrayed my trust (thereby impairing the reputation of the agency) and jeopardized my credit rating and privacy, but has hardly threatened the national security. Incumbents of these positions do not require a formal security clearance but must receive a cursory background investigation before performing their duties. This is officially known as a *suitability adjudication process*. They must complete a Standard Form (SF) 85, Questionnaire for Public Trust Positions, and undergo the investigation before assuming the duties. The investigation looks into the character of the applicant: are they reliable? Are they loyal to their country? Can they be trusted with information that is not available to the general public?

In those cases where disclosure of information could cause damage to national security, the qualifications for the incumbent must be at a higher bar. These are deemed *National Security* positions. Once again, the department or agency must determine the sensitivity level of information dissemination. If release could damage national security, the position is deemed *Confidential*; if damage would be serious, the position is considered *Secret*; if release would lead to exceptionally grave damage, then the position is deemed *Top Secret*.

Confidential-only clearances are relatively easy to obtain because no background investigation is necessary and the agency itself can perform the rudimentary search of public records to verify suitability of the applicant. However, individuals with Confidential-level approval have no access to Secret or Top Secret levels of information. Secret-level clearances do require a background investigation, yet the occupant does not have access to Top Secret information, but can access both Confidential and Secret levels. Those who hold Top Secret clearances may have access to all three levels.

The Department of Energy uses a different syntax for its clearances. L Clearance is analogous to Secret and Q Clearance is similar to Top Secret. Staff personnel for the president and vice president are subject to a "Yankee White"[10] clearance, which is also similar to Top Secret.

Most of these clearances have historically been issued by OPM. The others are issued by the Departments of Energy, Homeland Security, Justice, and State, as well as the CIA and NSA. Many of these clearances are transferable within a department or agency, following the individual as (s)he moves between offices. However, they often are not transferable between agencies—for example, the CIA may not recognize an FBI agent with the highest level of clearance granted by the Department of Justice. This creates a problem with sharing intelligence between agencies, which has received attention in

---

10. Special Access programs have a two-word nickname (or else a single code word). The process for selecting the code word for a given program is classified, primarily to avoid duplication. The actual words selected for a nickname come off a prescribed list but otherwise have no significance. Hence, the "Yankee White" designation for personal access to the president or vice president has nothing to do with a baseball team or color preference, nor any other hidden meaning.

the halls of Congress but still has not been resolved. Moreover, an initiative by the Trump administration to break apart OMB reflects the belief that DoD can investigate applicants more efficiently than OMB. Hence, as of October 1, 2019, DoD issues all clearances after investigation by the Defense Counterintelligence and Security Agency.[11]

Those who apply for these positions will first go through the usual screening interviews to see if their skills match the agency's need, and to identify any obvious showstoppers for a security clearance (such as a felony conviction or lack of citizenship, where such is required). Applicants for these positions must complete an SF-86, Questionnaire for National Security Positions, once approved to do so by their agency or company official. This can be done online using the Electronic Questionnaires for Investigations Processing (e-QIP) on a website operated by the National Background Investigations Bureau.[12] The questionnaire runs 121 pages, plus instructions and signature pages, so, yes, it will take some time to complete. Let's see what they want to know about the applicant:

- Every name used in the past. This presents a complication for spouses taking married names and any adopted children. All prior names and aliases must be provided and traced.
- Birth certificate information. A naturalized citizen must report country of origin, citizen and naturalization certification information. A foreign national must provide alien registration information. Passport or foreign identity card information must also be provided by all applicants.
- All residences within the past ten years, as well as neighbors within the past three years. Make sure you identify only those neighbors you get along with, or else embarrassing information could be revealed.
- All schools attended within the past ten years, along with a reference (such as a professor) for those attended within the past three years.
- Comprehensive employment history within the past ten years, including a supervisor reference for each. Any unemployment period must be reported with a contact person to verify same. If employment within the past seven years was terminated for misconduct, an explanation and person of contact must be reported.
- Any military history (including discharge status) and selective service registration, including any foreign nation's military service with persons of contact.

---

11. Executive Order 13869. See also Bur, "Security Clearance Agency Gets a New Name, Same Priorities," *Federal Times*.
12. https://nbib.opm.gov/e-qip-background-investigations/#url=Quick-Reference-Guide. A good primer for this subject is a Power Point presentation issued by OPM, "The Security Clearance and Investigation Process."

- Three personal references known over the past seven years. These are often friends, coworkers, and college roommates. Unlike the procedure in most federal job openings, these references will be contacted.
- Your spouse must be identified with any previous names and citizenship status. Divorce information must also be provided if applicable.
- Close relatives (parents, children, and in-laws) with citizenship, past names, current addresses, and employment data for each. The government does not normally ask for information on siblings.
- Any foreign citizens with whom you have an on-going relationship based on "affection, influence, common interests, and/or obligation" over the past seven years.[13] This also includes their address, prior names, basis of relationship, and frequency of contact. Don't forget any work colleagues who might not be U.S. citizens (I tripped up twice on this one because I did not know that two people I interacted with on the job were actually foreign citizens).
- Any foreign financial interest of the applicant or immediate family. Details must be reported such as dollar value and co-owner(s), any other tangible benefit (such as educational, medical, retirement, or any other social benefit), business venture, or conference or seminar.
- Any contact with a foreign government or representative, as well as any foreign national the applicant sponsored to visit the United States (such as a student, employee, or resident).
- Any political activity in a foreign country, as either a candidate or voter.
- All foreign travel within the past seven years, along with dates and destinations, and especially with any foreign government contacts. For those who take vacations overseas, or even a week on the beach in Mexico, this requires specific dates and locations.
- Any emotional or mental health issues within the past seven years, along with the health professionals contacted and treatment dates. Any court findings of mental incompetence must also be provided.
- Next comes the police record with any arrest or conviction within the past seven years, including any traffic citation over $300 (even if the charge was dropped). Special attention is paid to domestic abuse, drug or alcohol offenses, and firearms or explosives charges. Illegal use of drugs or other controlled substance will need to be reported; however, the government will not report this information to a law enforcement agency.[14] This includes abuse of prescription drugs and any counseling or treatment program. Alcohol use must be reported if it impacts work performance or required treatment.

---

13. General Services Administration, "SF-86 Questionnaire for National Security Positions," 59.

14. Note that possession or use of marijuana in any form is illegal under federal law, regardless of its purpose (even medicinal) and even though it is legal in many states. See Controlled Substances Act of 1970, 84 Stat. 1236 and 21 U.S.C. 801. Its use may be held against the applicant.

- All prior clearance requests and adjudications.
- The financial section of the questionnaire focuses on bankruptcy, gambling, failure to file or pay taxes or alimony, credit card misuse or counseling, financial judgments, repossessions, loan defaults, references to a collection agency, credit card suspension, eviction, wage garnishment, or debt delinquency of four months or more.
- Any illegal access to an information system within the past seven years or any data modification, destruction, or unauthorized use/addition/deletion of hardware or software/media.
- Details if a party to any civil action within the past ten years.
- Membership in a terrorist organization or one geared to overthrow the U.S. government (and is a certain cause for a negative adjudication). This includes any organization that threatens use of force to discourage others from exercising their constitutional rights.

The investigation process takes months because several law enforcement agencies must be contacted (federal, state, and local, based upon where the applicant lived or went to school within the past ten years) and their answers awaited and then analyzed. If no answer is received from a particular source agency, the clearance analyst must contact that agency and pursue an answer (thereby causing another delay). Fingerprints must be run through a verification system, either electronically or by paper submission, so if the fingers were not properly rolled during the printing process, it may need to be repeated. National agency record checks are necessary to identify any known felons or candidates with dubious backgrounds (e.g., repetitive driving violations, gambling habits, or drug violations). Every previous address must be verified and local police offices contacted, so people who have moved around will take longer to investigate. Former names and schools attended must also be thoroughly checked out. Foreign citizens must be verified with a check to the Immigration and Naturalization Service. Foreign travel often adds to the delay in processing because each instance must be examined. Past employers must also be contacted and evaluated. This impacted me because I worked my way through college as a member of a labor union: this association delayed my initial clearance adjudication for a month while the union was checked out for any subversive activities (and it did have an ancient history of Communist Party membership).

The background investigations are done by National Background Investigations Bureau within OMB by contract employees.[15] Civil servants facing a first-

---

15. The Nuclear Regulatory Commission runs its own investigations and adjudications for its employees and contractors. Other departments which may conduct their own investigations are State, Treasury, Homeland Security, and the FBI. Under the new clearance process, the Department of Defense may eventually gain control of all investigations and adjudications.

time clearance review are subject to an advanced national agency check with inquiries, while all first-time and repeat applicants (civil service, contractor, and military) are subject to a national agency check with law and credit agencies. The investigators contact several law enforcement agencies (federal, state, and local) and credit agencies. Past and present addresses and foreign travel destinations are also checked out and verified. If the individual is targeted for a low risk position, then a clean report is usually enough for a clearance up to a Secret level. If the position involves Moderate risk, then a Personal Subject Interview will be conducted, with inquiries sent to employers, references, and schools (within the past five years) that are listed on the SF-86. Again, if these sources check out, then the clearance is granted.[16] Of course, if it is later found that the applicant lied on the SF-86, it is grounds for immediate termination.

A personal interview is necessary to uncover and clear up inconsistencies. Interviews will also be held with past (within the recent ten years) and present coworkers, neighbors, professors, and supervisors, as well as the personal references provided by the applicant. After all information is received and analyzed, the analyst must then review the information against adjudicative guidelines and a recommendation to a supervisor for final adjudication.[17] These guidelines include:[18]

- allegiance to the United States, as opposed to foreign influence or preference. Dual citizenship is acceptable so long as the United States is one of them and the individual places this country's interests above all others. This is why U.S. citizenship is often a mandatory requirement for a clearance;
- criminal conduct. The government does not employ unpunished felons;
- emotional, mental, and personality disorders, since they could impact job performance;
- financial difficulties. A defaulting mortgage or excessive credit card debt could indicate unreliability and a need to engage in illegal activity to escape financial ruin;
- outside activities, if they raise a red flag in one's personal behavior;
- personal conduct. This covers consumption of alcohol and drugs because dependency often impacts job performance;
- security violations, including misuse of information systems. Such behavior would eventually lead to dismissal, so previous experiences could indicate a negative pattern of behavior; and
- sexual behavior, since this could lead to compromise and hence blackmail.

---

16. An excellent source of information about the various levels of review is http://fedcas.com/wp-content/uploads/2012/05/Federal-Suitability-Security-Clearance-Chart.pdf.

17. Office of the Director of National Intelligence, "Security Executive Agent Directive 4."

18. Office of Personnel Management, "The Security Clearance and Investigation Process," 16, and Executive Order 12968.

The applicant will be advised of any negative finding along with reason(s) for rejection. However, there are mitigating circumstances of a specific conduct which could permit issuance of a clearance even upon a negative finding:[19]

- age and maturity of the individual,
- circumstances,
- frequency and timeframe,
- knowledgeable participation,
- level of coercion or exploitation,
- likelihood of continuation or recurrence,
- motivation for the conduct,
- nature and extent,
- presence or absence of rehabilitation and other permanent behavioral changes, and
- seriousness.

Top Secret positions require more than this, however. In addition to all the above, the applicant will be subject to a *Single Scope Background Investigation*, a more in-depth analysis going back up to 15 years. Other positions may require a *Full Scope Background Investigation* which involves psychological questions for the applicant, such as whether (s)he ever cheated on a college exam.

Some positions require applicants to undergo a polygraph examination, which is designed to focus on either counterintelligence capability or else the applicant's lifestyle. *Polygraphs*, more familiarly known as lie detectors, are procedures in which a subject wears a blood pressure cuff and is asked a series of questions which can only be answered by Yes or No. The effectiveness of polygraph testing is very controversial.[20] It is used frequently by law enforcement agencies to investigate criminal activity, with some success (as demonstrated in the many police detective series we all see on television). However, its usefulness in general background investigations is more controversial. The National Academy of Sciences report on this subject concluded:[21]

> Because actual screening applications involve considerably more ambiguity for the examinee and in determining truth that arises in specific-incident studies, polygraph accuracy for screening purposes is almost certainly lower than what can be achieved by specific-incident polygraph tests in the field.

---

19. Office of Personnel Management, "The Security Clearance and Investigation Process," 17.
20. National Academy of Sciences, *The Polygraph and Lie Detection.*
21. National Academy of Sciences, *The Polygraph and Lie Detection*, 4.

The entire laborious process takes several months for a Secret clearance investigation, and often a year or more for Top Secret clearances. The backlog of requested clearances and updates can run into the hundreds of thousands at any one time. Quality sometimes suffers and cost goes up. As a result, the government is implementing a new initiative known as Trusted Workforce 2.0 to promote use of automation rather than paperwork, investigations already performed by other authorized investigation agencies, and greater clearance portability between agencies for employees who move between agencies or contractors. This process is just beginning to be implemented as this book is written, so no feedback as to results is available yet.

Although Top Secret is the highest level of clearance, it is not the highest level of information control. Some information is deemed *Sensitive Compartmented Information (SCI)* which is involved with *Special Access Programs (SAP)*. Access is restricted to those with a need to know, not merely because they have a certain security level. This information will be classified as either Secret or Top Secret but carries the additional SCI designation. Even if the individual has a Top Secret clearance and the information is deemed Secret SCI, the person cannot obtain access to the information without an additional SCI endorsement. Of course, an individual cleared at SECRET/SCI has no access to TOP SECRET information regardless of whether (s)he is SCI-protected.

These SAPs are branded with code names which are simplified into three-letter trigraph designations. So a program with the codename HURRAH (which I doubt is a real name) could have a trigraph of HUR. All data generated by or passing through this program will be stamped with a security clearance level and this trigraph.

Applicants for positions requiring SCI access undergo the same process as Top Secret candidates, though additional investigation and adjudication may be required. Often, this means a polygraph examination and sometimes a psychological evaluation. For this reason, their position is referred to as "TS/SCI." Whoever owns the SCI information will then grant access to the compartment or subcompartment. The clearance does not specify the compartment(s) accessed because such knowledge, when combined with the candidate's resume, could reveal sensitive information.

No individual can apply on his/her own initiative for a security clearance. (S)he must be sponsored by a government agency or contractor for a known position that requires such a clearance. Each agency or contractor has a security officer who can submit the paperwork and track its progress for the application process. A clearance request can be submitted for a prospective employee, who then goes about his/her daily activities with a current employer until adjudication is complete. If selected, the individual is given 30 days to report for work or else forfeit the offer. Interim clearances can be granted by an agency if they are confident that the employee will pass a formal investigation.

A Top Secret clearance is good for five years, a Secret clearance is good for ten years, and a Confidential or Public Trust clearance is good for 15 years. About a year before expiration, the process must be renewed and the individual must prepare a new SF-86 and a periodic reinvestigation must be conducted. If a clearance has not been renewed for whatever reason (such as assuming a new position which does not require a clearance), it can nonetheless be renewed for a period of up to 24 months without a new investigation. Regardless, access to a SAP is terminated upon losing the need to know, regardless of the status of one's clearance.

Many agencies allow certain employees with active clearances to keep them even after they leave the government. These employees are usually high-ranking officials who maintain institutional memory and can thus advise current government employees and managers. For instance, past CIA directors routinely maintain their clearances for life. Of course, they must still undergo periodic reinvestigation to keep their clearances current.

Any cleared employee or contractor must sign a non-disclosure agreement with the agency to protect all classified information from unauthorized use or disclosure. This also applies when classified information is inadvertently disclosed, such as when somebody stumbles upon information they are not cleared to see.

Nobody knows for sure how extensive the "black world" really is. A two-year investigation by the *Washington Post* uncovered 1,271 government agencies and nearly 2,000 contractors, spanning roughly 10,000 locations.[22] Their research shows 854,000 people hold Top Secret clearances—these do not include people with only Secret or lower-level clearances (such as Public Trust). They estimate that 17 million square feet of building space devoted to top secret intelligence work have been constructed in the Washington, D.C., area just since the 9/11 terrorist attacks.[23] Some 50,000 intelligence reports are generated each year, with an incredible amount of overlap, inefficiency, and waste of manpower and money. The total budget is unknown, although the *Post* investigation found $75 billion. The National Security Agency alone processes 1.7 billion pieces of communications every day. Yet current employees will not speak of the matter because they are prohibited by their non-disclosure agreement, or else fear retribution.

---

22. Priest and Arkin, "A Hidden World, Growing beyond Control," *Washington Post*. The results are based on public information and interviews with former employees. This article is from 2010, indicating that the numbers have only grown over time.

23. For this intelligence discussion, I am bounding the Washington area by Baltimore/Washington International Thurgood Marshall Airport (BWI) to the north; Linthicum, Maryland, to the east; Quantico Marine Base (and associated tenant activities) to the south; and Leesburg, Virginia, to the west.

And the construction continues throughout the country. Department of Homeland Security is building its headquarters seven miles east of the Pentagon, the only larger office building in the Washington area. The headquarters is on the site of St. Elizabeth's Hospital, a former mental institute with grand yet aging brick buildings. This initiative will consolidate a number of its agencies into one area (the U.S. Coast Guard moved its offices there several years ago), thereby reducing office rental costs and the need to transport people around the area for meetings. Unfortunately, development is dragging and the economically deprived neighborhood discourages commuters: there is no dedicated subway stop and the shuttle bus service operates on half hours during off-peak hours (more often during peak hours).

Highly classified work is normally done within a *Special Compartmentalized Industrial Facility* (*SCIF*). These areas are specially built with sheathing around the walls to prevent eavesdropping by outside entities. Entry to a SCIF requires a special badge, a passcode entry on a keypad, sometimes a retinal scan, lockers to store cell phones (which are strictly forbidden inside because they can transmit signals to the outside), briefcase inspections and x-ray machines, and ever-present security guards with unsmiling "game faces." Their size varies, however. I attended meetings regularly in one SCIF which was no more than a briefing room, maybe 20 feet by 40 feet. Others are the size of football fields.

Many employees working in this environment are low-paid analysts who make $40,000 to $65,000 per year, crunching mountains of data every day to learn what is going on in their world. Often their reports add nothing to the body of knowledge, merely rehash that which is already known. But there are times when their efforts pay off in thwarting a terrorist plot or heading off a military or political crisis. In these times, they provide a major service to the country.

The *Post* investigation also uncovered a Department of Defense list of SAP code names that runs for 300 pages. Just because you have a clearance does not mean you have a need to know, and it is not uncommon for only one person in a workgroup to have that access. Cleared personnel often cannot share their information with colleagues, subordinates, or even supervisors. Many a support contractor cannot discuss the job with his/her own supervisor because the latter is not cleared to the same program as the employee. I personally saw an Army lieutenant general (with three stars) blow up and storm out of a meeting because he was not cleared to obtain an answer to his question. Yet the employee who was the subject of his anger was well within his nondisclosure obligation to refuse to answer him. The chain of command can suffer sometimes because of this process, but that is just too bad for the offended party.

Chapter 7

Contractors

Roughly four million contractors work for the federal government. During the height of our Afghan and Iraqi involvement during the Bush administration, the number of contractors was closer to five million. That number dropped significantly during the Obama administration, but has gone up again due to border security and wall construction under the Trump administration. Once we pull out of Afghanistan and Iraq, contractors will number again around 3 or 3.5 million.

Contractors cannot perform *inherently governmental functions*. Agencies decide what tasks are entailed in this term, subject to OMB approval. Examples of these functions include efforts to:[1]

- administer public trusts;
- approve agency responses to Freedom of Information Act requests;
- approve federal inspections and licenses;
- ascertain agency or foreign policy and application of regulations;
- award and administer contracts;
- collect, control, and disburse public funds (unless authorized by statute);[2]
- command military forces;
- conduct administrative hearings to determine eligibility for a security clearance or participation in government programs;
- conduct criminal investigations;
- control Treasury accounts;
- decide budget policy and strategy;
- decide government property disposition;

---

1. Lindner, 59–60.
2. Exceptions are concession sales or examining vouchers and invoices, which are not considered to be inherently governmental in nature.

- decide whether contract costs are reasonable, allocable, and allowable;
- determine federal program priorities for budget requests;
- determine what supplies or services are to be acquired by the government;
- direct and control federal employees;
- direct intelligence and counter-intelligence operations;
- draft testimony and correspondence responses to Congress or a federal auditor;
- interview and select individuals for federal government employment;
- perform prosecutions and adjudications;
- ratify position descriptions and performance standards for federal employees;
- terminate contracts; and
- vote on any source selection boards or performance evaluation boards.

Examples of functions that are not generally considered to be inherently governmental functions, but which might come close to crossing the line, include:

- acquisition planning;
- budget preparation;
- developing regulations or statements of work;
- feasibility studies and strategy options to develop policy;
- policy interpretation (e.g., attending conferences on an agency's behalf or conducting agency training courses or community relations campaigns); and
- preparing responses to Freedom of Information Act requests.

In addition to manufacturing contracts to build hardware, contractors also provide services to the federal government. A *service contract* directly engages the time and effort of a contractor to perform an identifiable task rather than to furnish an end item of supply.[3] A service contract can cover services performed by either professional or nonprofessional personnel on an individual or organizational basis. Some areas in which service contracts are found include:

- advice and assistance;
- architect-engineering;
- communications;
- housekeeping and base support;
- modernization, modification, overhaul, rehabilitation, repair, salvage, or servicing of equipment, supplies, or systems;
- operation of government-owned equipment, real property, and systems;

---

3. FAR 37.1. See also Lindner, 164–66.

- recurring maintenance of real property;
- research and development; and
- transportation.

As a special type of service, a *personal services contract* is characterized by the employer-employee relationship it creates between the customer and the contractor's personnel. Such a relationship occurs under a service contract when, as a result of contract terms or the manner of administration during performance, contractor personnel are subject to the relatively continuous supervision and control of a customer officer or employee.

The very nature of a personal services contract is inherently a real problem in federal contracting. The government is required to obtain its employees by direct hire. Obtaining personal services by contract circumvents those laws unless Congress has specifically authorized acquisition of the services through contracting. Hence, agencies do not award personal services contracts unless specifically authorized by statute. However, giving an order for a specific item or service, with the right to reject the finished product or result, is an acceptable action. Examples of situations which raise the specter of personal services include:

- comparable services that meet similar needs performed in the same or similar agencies using civil service personnel;
- performance on site;
- services integral to the agency mission;
- the nature of the service or its performance requires government direction or supervision of contractor employees to retain government control of the function;
- the need for the service is expected to last beyond one year; or
- tools and equipment are furnished by the government.

On-site performance is an especially tricky situation. Government personnel must respect the need for distance between themselves and contractor employees. Even though many service contracts require on-site performance (especially where access to classified information is regularly required), it still presents an easy opportunity for government personnel to "cross the line" and provide personal direction contrary to the arm's-length distance they are required to obey. This problem can best be avoided through constant vigilance by supervisors and the contracting officer.

Contracting officers may enter into contracts with temporary help service firms for the brief use of private sector temporaries. These services are not regarded as personal services but cannot be used in lieu of recruitment under civil service laws or to displace a federal employee.

Any instance where the government requires the contractor to provide advice, analyses, ideas, opinions, recommendations, or reports could influence the accountability, authority, and responsibilities of government officials. Hence, agencies must again ensure that qualified government employees oversee contractor activities, especially to support government policy or decision making. All contract personnel who attend meetings and answer government telephones, and whose contractor status is not obvious to third parties, must identify themselves as contractors to avoid creating an impression that they are government officials, unless the agency decides that no harm can come if they fail to identify themselves. The government ensures that all documents or reports produced by contractors are marked as contractor products.

Agencies may contract for *advisory and assistance services* to obtain:[4]

- advice regarding developments in foundation, industry, or university research;
- operational support and improvement of an organization or its hardware or managerial systems;
- opinions, skills, or special knowledge of noted experts;
- outside points of view to avoid too-limited judgment on critical issues; or
- understanding of, and developing alternative solutions to, complex issues.

The acquisition office is the focal point to handle each procurement action. This office hosts the contracting officer, negotiator, legal counsel, and small business specialist.[5] The requiring activity or program will provide the program manager and technical representative, and its cognizant finance office will furnish the comptroller both to certify availability of funds and to provide the accounting data against which the contractor will be paid.

The *Contracting Officer* is a federal employee who is authorized to award and administer contracts on behalf of the United States. This official receives a warrant (suitable for framing) from the agency head which sets forth any limitations on authority, such as dollar threshold of obligation. The contracting officer has the warrant to commit the government, leads the negotiation team, and serves as business manager for the acquisition. (S)he bears great latitude to exercise business judgment and maintain fairness and integrity of the acquisition process, and has the authority to determine the application of rules, regulations, and policies to a specific contract. Contracting officers are selected based on their experience in government or commercial contracting

---

4. Federal Acquisition Regulatory Council, *Federal Acquisition Regulation (FAR)*, see FAR 37.2.
5. Lindner, 38–41.

and administration, education (e.g., accounting, business administration, law, or engineering), and training in acquisition courses. Some military personnel also hold warrants as part of their work duties.

Contracting officers often have assistants (often called *procurement analysts* or similar nomenclature) who develop documentation, develop solicitations, analyze cost and pricing data, assist in negotiations and source selection activities, and handle a myriad of other tasks. These are usually civil servants or contract employees, and provide an environment to develop future contracting officers.

All acquisition officials, especially contracting officers, must meet education and training standards established by the department or agency.[6] Undergoing extensive training for the position, the contracting officer must have the personality and experience to work with technical personnel, yet reports along a separate chain of command. Key traits for the contracting officer are:

- ability to perceive and exploit power;
- analytical capability of contractor accounting and purchasing systems, and all cost and pricing issues;
- communicating effectively as a government spokesman;
- knowledge of acquisition laws and regulations;
- knowledge of economic and market conditions, and the industry and product/service;
- mathematical analytic techniques (e.g., learning curves, regression, and correlation);
- performance measurability;
- planning ability; and
- sound judgment and common sense.

Advisory and assistance services are quite common within the federal government to obtain expertise not available within the civil service. There is nothing inherently wrong with this process, as long as it is not abused. Managers should accept their input courteously and weigh it in making their decisions. Employees should interact with such consultants as necessary, giving them a wide berth to do their job, while maintaining an arms-length distance. Unfortunately, I have seen many civil servants who treat contractors with disdain, resenting that they are needed in the first place.

---

6. DoD has taken the lead in establishing such standards to comply with 10 USC 87 Defense Acquisition Workforce Improvement Act (DAWIA). However, all federal departments and agencies with procurement authority have established their own program of on-the-job professionalism.

*   *   *

Lesson #20: Civil servants and contractors should treat each other with respect but not coziness.

*   *   *

Of course, this disdain does not reflect reality and comes from a lack of understanding of the situation. I have also seen personal resentment by civil servants over the pay level and manner of dress of contractors. In point of fact, contractors often dress better and more conservatively because they cannot afford to offend their customer with any article of clothing that might be deemed offensive, whereas civil servants often have more latitude in how casually they may dress. It may be true that a support contract employee may be paid five percent more than the civil servant sitting at the next cubicle; however, it is pretty certain that (s)he does not receive comparable health, leave, pension, and retirement benefits.

There is also a raging argument over the concept of paying contractor employees by the hour, rather than for results. I have always believed that results are more important than hours worked, but I suspect that I am in the minority on this point. So many federal managers are suspicious that contractors may not be giving their best effort and padding their hours that they insist that the contractors sit with them in the office, record their hours by submitting timesheets, and get paid by the hour. That way, the managers can keep an eye on them. I have also seen federal managers who pay contractors to sit in the office full-time for their availability, to be consulted as needed, even if they only put in a few meaningful hours of work per week. This is not a desirable situation, but I have seen it happen more times than I care to count.

Similarly, telecommuting is another controversial subject in government performance, especially in terms of contractor performance and government oversight. Government managers will disagree on whether contract workers can be allowed to perform from home or a nearby telework center, or whether they must sit in government-owned or rented spaces (which are not free and raise the specter of personal services). It is the rare enlightened federal manager who will allow contractor personnel to work from their corporate office, or even from home, rather than be under their constant supervision. Congress has stepped into this dispute by prohibiting an agency from discouraging a contractor who wishes to allow its employees to telecommute in the performance of government contracts.[7] However, the contracting officer can determine that the requirements of the agency, such as frequent meetings or security requirements, cannot be met if telecommuting is permitted.[8] There

---

7. National Defense Authorization Act, Section 1428, 41 U.S.C. 403.
8. FAR 7.108 and Lindner, 208.

is no current program for either the government or the contractor to either encourage or discourage telecommuting among contract employees. It is quite a conundrum that the manager insists on having contractor support, yet doesn't trust them. But this is reality and happens every day in federal offices across the land. Since the contractor must play ball with the federal manager or risk losing the contract, (s)he will go along with this arrangement.

If a contractor will have routine physical access to a federally controlled facility and/or information system during performance, the contract will contain provisions to comply with Federal Information Processing Standards Publication (FIPS PUB) Number 201, "Personal Identity Verification of Federal Employees and Contractors," and OMB Guidance M-05-24, "Implementation of Homeland Security Presidential Directive (HSPD) 12-Policy for a Common Identification Standard for Federal Employees and Contractors."[9,10] This is why employees and contractors wear badges which are plainly visible above the waist (not hooked onto the belt) and which are often color-coded to show to which areas they can and cannot gain admittance. Often, contractor badges have a special marking to distinguish them from civil servants.

Agency procedures often require that the contractor account for all government personal identity cards or badges issued to its employees, and to return them upon contract completion or employee departure.[11] If the contractor fails to do so, final payment may be withheld.

Government personnel do have certain obligations in terms of dealing with contractors. It is best for program managers for both the agency and the contractor to hold formal regular meetings to address contract performance and assign new tasks. The contracting officer has a technical representative (*COTR*) who must ensure that any tasks assigned to the contractor stay within the scope of the contract. I once worked on a contract where the COTR broke this rule by changing her position day-by-day and assigning us tasks well outside the scope of work which our team was not qualified to perform. Our company formally complained to the contracting officer, and she rescinded the COTR's letter of authority.

The COTR cannot get directly involved with the hiring process but can interview applicants and state whether they are or are not acceptable for performance under the current contract. Nor can any government employee get involved in establishing the work schedule for an individual contact employee, though they can define the parameters of a workday within the office.

---

9. Federal Information Processing Standards Publication (FIPS PUB) Number 201, "Personal Identity Verification of Federal Employees and Contractors." See also Lindner, 65–66.

10. Office of Management and Budget Guidance M-05-24, "Implementation of Homeland Security Presidential Directive (HSPD) 12-Policy for a Common Identification Standard for Federal Employees and Contractors."

11. FAR 4.13.

So the government can say that contract coverage is required between 8:00 and 4:30, but may run into legal hurdles if they say that a specific contract employee cannot stay late on his/her own time, nor take the morning off for a medical appointment (unless the individual must attend a specific meeting related to contract performance, for example).

Most agencies have rules to deal with personal relationships between government and contractor personnel. If a government employee is retiring or celebrating a birthday or anniversary, a contract employee may attend only on personal time, not billable time. If the opposite situation occurs, where a government employee wants to attend a contract employee's function, (s)he usually must get a supervisor's approval to avoid the appearance of favoritism. The way to handle this situation is to formally acknowledge the presence of a casual relationship, such as church membership or youth sports. Romantic relationships should be avoided at all costs, since they can get very complicated in terms of apparent favoritism. Moreover, any gifts provided to the host or beneficiary are limited to a nominal value of $20 (including a gift certificate). It is also expected (but by no means always done) where a basket is prominently placed so that a contract employee can deposit money to pay for the cost of attendance to avoid the appearance of receiving a gift from the government.

Speaking of gifts, managers are prohibited from soliciting gifts from employees, since it could create a performance rating issue for any employee who declines to participate. This does not prevent an employee from voluntarily creating a fund drive to buy a gift for a manager's landmark occasion, such as a wedding or birth. This is best done by posting a flyer and stating who is collecting the money. Contractors may voluntarily contribute to such a fund, but cannot be solicited or encouraged to give, again to maintain an arms-length relationship.

Finally, a word seems appropriate about a new trend among contractor personnel. Some companies dispatch, or train consultants already under contract, to become *thought leaders* to advocate initiatives that reflect their areas of expertise. They often speak at professional and public meetings. This is fine as long as everybody understands the hidden agenda here. Their employer is in business to make money and is promoting a service in an area of expertise that is their specialty and therefore ripe for contract coverage. Thought leadership is all about creating a demand for the company's ideas and may cross the line into pure marketing. The audience should indeed pay attention to their advocacy and incorporate it into their knowledge base and planning, but should not fall into the trap of blindly adopting the company behind the message without searching for alternative approaches.

Chapter 8

Staff Work

Staff work addresses the day-to-day operational and administrative needs of an organization. It provides a two-way information flow between the commanding office and field operations. A good staffer also filters information for the commander so (s)he is not burdened by issues of lower significance and can focus on big-picture issues.

Staff offices focus on mission, functional areas of responsibility, compliance with law, and developing policy and regulations. Secretarial staff duties include such areas as operations, training, logistics, C4I (command control, communications, computers, and intelligence), information operations, and resource management (both financial and personnel). The department or agency head will have a chief of staff (in the military it is often an executive officer) to direct the tasks of staff members and ensure their coordination, such that their activities are carried out promptly and efficiently. They must provide the decision-maker with accurate and timely relevant information and thorough recommendations.

Staff work is much less structured than operational work. You never know when you go to work what the day will bring, so a staffer must be able to adjust focus quickly and roll with the punches. A staffer must learn to cope with ambiguity.

When it comes to describing the activities and values of a good staffer, once again DoD leads the way. Army Field Manual 22-100 discusses the attributes and skills expected of all staff members and leaders.[1] As Army leaders, staff officers are expected to possess and develop those characteristics;

---

1. Headquarters, Department of the Army, "Field Manual 22-100: Army Leadership–Be, Know, Do." See also "Field Manual 6-0: Mission Command: Command and Control of Army Forces, Appendix C Staff Organization and Staff Officers."

however, staff work requires specialized applications of them. A good staff officer is a team player who demonstrates the following:

- communication skills,
- competence,
- confidence,
- flexibility,
- initiative,
- loyalty, and
- managerial ability.

Good communications skills lead to clearly articulated delivery of information both orally and in writing. These writings include briefings, orders, plans, reports, and studies. They must be concise and clearly understandable by decision-makers who have no time to decipher vague wording. Proper use of charts and graphs can be of great help here, which means that effective use of applications such as Microsoft PowerPoint, Project, and Visio are crucial to success.

Above all, good staffers are competent in their areas of expertise. They must have to ability to research and issue and develop creative and well-considered solutions. The analysis cannot be biased and must consider all aspects of the problem. They must also be aware of how staff integration should occur, both horizontally and vertically. They must also be willing to admit when they do not know the answer but do know where to go to find the best answer.

*   *   *

Lesson #21: Anticipate your manager's needs.

*   *   *

The best staffers have the ability to anticipate their manager's needs (and his or her higher manager's needs) and program requirements. Develop answers *before* questions are asked. The best staffers take advantage of every opportunity they can find to solve problems before they become problems. Conducting "what-if" thought experiments in your spare time, such as while commuting, is one way to address upcoming needs. I did this regularly and avoided many a surprise on the job.

Time management is crucial because it affects the staffer, colleagues, and subordinates. Reasonable suspense dates must be set based on relative priorities of each task. Further, the staffer must properly manage resources to avoid waste and duplication of effort.

Staffers cannot complete their work alone. They must consult and cooperate with other managers and colleagues. They cannot afford to behave as if they know it all; input from staff specialists is essential to flesh out ideas and show management that all readily available resources have been used. Individual interests must yield to the best interests of the organization to ensure cooperation and coordination.

The most dreaded part of staff work is the *data call*. Some higher-up or member of Congress wants information on some subject unexpectedly, which requires research and gathering data from multiple sources. Many times, these sources are deployed nationwide or even worldwide, so e-mails and phone calls crisscross the airwaves. The requestor wants the answer immediately (*as soon as possible*, or *ASAP*), long before the information is collected. Once the data call is received, the information must be collected, analyzed, and assessed for findings and recommendations. And of course, each step in this process adds delays to the response time of Congressional inquiries. My time on staff saw deadlines routinely violated and response times turn into several weeks. Ensuring that the laws of the land are faithfully executed brings with it a boatload of issues, time delays, and effort. And it is difficult to hold any one person responsible or accountable for these issues, since so many hands touch the data call and response.

Obviously, information flow is critical to staff offices. Accurate and timely information must flow in three different directions: horizontally across functional areas and colleagues, vertically upward to senior management, and vertically downward to lower-tier units and field offices. Staff offices usually (but not always) learn first of emerging issues and must be prepared to notify upper management of major impacts on agency operations. However, care must be taken not to burden management with small matters that can be safely handled at a lower level. This is why more experienced analysts supervise sections comprised of less-experienced staff aides. The latter collect and analyze data and make recommendations, while the senior staffers review their work, return for revision if necessary, and submit the final product to management for approval.

Many people make a career out of staff work, often because it is less stressful than operations. However, choosing this path may lead them to lose touch with operational conditions and considerations, as well as being out of the loop in highly technical arenas. For these reasons, rotation from staff back into operations is often a good idea. The military does this religiously, limiting staff tours to two or three years at most. I always regretted that civilian positions on staff are permanent without the opportunity to rotate back into "the real world." I once worked with someone who had made a career out of staff work, spending only her first few months in a low-level operational environment (which she did not enjoy). When her boss told her several years later that she had peaked in her promotion potential and needed a return to operations to enhance her chances, she promptly sought out and obtained another staff position in another department. She was not interested in leaving staff work, even for higher pay. I worked with another person, in the private sector, whose sole goal was to be an executive assistant because she wanted to be physically near the center of decision-making. Again, she left our organization for a lower-paying executive assistant position at another firm, just to sit near the company president.

Staff work involves studying a problem and providing a series of options, along with a recommendation for action. The staffer records the research done, facts collected, analysis performed on alternative courses of action, and recommendations. This process will normally take about a week. Ideally, the decision maker merely has to sign off on the recommendation, rather than helping the staffer work the problem.

Upon receiving an assignment, the staffer must first understand a number of things about it:

- the deadline,
- experts on staff,
- format of the final product (where to find a sample),
- frequency of updates to boss,
- motivations and emotions of the decision-maker,
- parameters (financial, geographic, and public considerations and timeliness),
- purpose and importance,
- resources needed to complete,
- reviewers' list,
- scope of impact, and
- your own knowledge/skills/abilities.

The inexperienced staffer will ask the boss for help—often feeling frustrated, but this is not the approach and/or reaction that the boss wants to see. Rather, (s)he wants you to do the research and create prudent solutions, working out any details toward selection and implementation. This is another reason why staff specialists should be consulted during this process, including outside experts.

*   *   *

Lesson #22: Take solutions to your boss—not questions.

*   *   *

The staffer must advise the boss what to do, not ask the boss what to do. This is the mistake of an inexperienced staff aide and will not long be tolerated by a busy executive. The staff aide should study and write (usually in many drafts) until a best course of action emerges. That is the option to be recommended to the boss for approval.

* * *

Lesson #23: Develop confidence in what you are selling.

* * *

By confidently telling the truth about what you are selling, you will have nothing to hide and become transparent to your audience. Most decision-makers want to buy a solution to their needs or problems, and therefore look forward to your presentation. They will also appreciate a problem-solver who has done some homework to understand their needs and wants. So, you want to make their job easier by honestly and openly providing a solution that gives them what they want.

* * *

Lesson #24: How will it look in the *Washington Post*?

* * *

Be aware of political ramifications of your advice. Any decision that appears on its face to be sound can nonetheless be twisted by those with a different agenda to look like a misguided, terrible, or even wasteful idea. Critics abound at every turn. To avoid this, take a moment to adopt a contrarian view. Act as a devil's advocate to find any weaknesses in your position or decision. Then make any necessary adjustments to overcome such objections.

When advancing your idea, first anticipate the reception it will get from management. The staffer should be aware of internal and external issues that will affect and be affected by the action to be taken. Research into the surrounding environment as part of the issue development process will alert the savvy staffer to consider the impact of any implementation on others.

When acting in place of your boss, a full report to their supervisor is absolutely essential to provide continuity of operations. Staffers must disclose the full story to their manager, including facts that may not be what the manager wants to hear, both good and bad news. Remember that real people will be affected by the decision ultimately made.

* * *

Lesson #25: Keep stakeholders informed, not surprised.

* * *

Your boss is certainly a key figure in any issue resolution. You do not want him or her to be uninformed, especially in a meeting—an embarrassed boss reflects poorly on the staff aide and could lead to an undesirable job transfer. The list of reviewers must also be clued in to what is going on so they are kept informed. In my time on the staff, we called this a *chop list* because we required each reviewer to initial a routing sheet on the cover of the memorandum to show that they had reviewed and concurred in the proposed course of action. A gatekeeper in the approving official's front office would review the list to ensure that all initials were present and would return it to the staffer if even one was missing. Every *stakeholder* (one who is affected by the decision) must be contacted and afforded the opportunity to comment, if only to avoid surprises. As one senior officer told me, "I only like surprises on Christmas morning."

Now that you have scoped out the process to go through, the next step is to collect and analyze data. This is time-consuming and will undoubtedly irk those parties who look for a quick solution or an already-favored position. But it is critical to good staff work to thoroughly research an issue from all angles to unearth all relevant facts and opinions.

*   *   *

Lesson #26: Avoid the easy way out—it's often the wrong way out.

*   *   *

Start with looking at the background and history of the issue. Is this the first time it has been examined? If not, find who looked at it before and ask them for their experiences and findings when looking at the issue. This is the best time to interview the stakeholder(s). Some of them may be subject matter experts who can provide valuable insight into the issue. Performing due diligence is absolutely crucial to good staff work.

I reviewed the business plan to comply with a foreign agreement to dredge a port in Morocco to accommodate ocean-going naval vessels. This required entering into contract with the Port Authority of Morocco, who in turn would obtain the necessary contractors to perform the dredging. The contacting officer developed a list of about 45 clauses that were standard in defense contracting that he wanted to be waived from the contract with the Port Authority. I was instantly turned off by such a massive request for waivers, and called in the contract negotiator to explain himself. He sheepishly said that he had not discussed the issue with Morocco, but was merely requesting waivers in case they were necessary. I was dismayed that he had not even tried to discuss the issue and denied his request, other than to waive two clauses we routinely waived with foreign firms. As it turned out, they were able to negotiate a fair deal with all the normal clauses in place and no need for further waivers. The easy way out for the contracting officer would have left us with significant reductions in our rights.

* * *

Lesson #27: You can't be an expert on everything.

* * *

Analyzing the results of this investigation should identify any gaps in the body of known facts and any weaknesses in previously held theories. Be sure to document both your input and your analysis. This effort should reveal the root cause(s) of the issue. Avoid emotion or prejudice from coloring your evaluation. Gap analysis may be useful to identify the difference(s) between the current state of reality and the desired end state. The various options could be evaluated quantitatively by a rating system or qualitatively by discussing the relative merits and drawbacks of each option. Make sure the recommendation for any recommended course of action is fully justified.

* * *

Lesson #28: Emphasize value, not cost.

* * *

The most common evaluation criteria are cost and policy compliance. Lower-cost alternatives are often favorable to a decision-maker, especially if budget constraints are present. Of course, low cost alone should never be the sole criterion for a decision unless multiple options are otherwise comparable. Recurring costs are also significant because they have long-term budgetary impacts. And hiring more people to fix a problem has long-term implications because salary levels continue to rise every year with wage escalation factors.

Nevertheless, even if your solution is expensive in terms of initial outlay, you must emphasize its *value* to the decision-makers. They are looking at return on investment rather than upfront cost. Moreover, the best solution may be the one with long-term benefits rather than short-term gains. Hence, you are not just selling a solution—you are selling an investment.

Now it is time to draft your report. This gets pretty complicated when a task group is working on a project, since all members must agree on both the final recommendation(s) and the language within the final report. Consensus is often not easy. This may lead to multiple rounds of draft reviews and updates, until hopefully all parties reach agreement. Beware of members who wordsmith every paragraph, since they can produce bottlenecks and turn off other members. Minority reports may be generated, even when the parties agree on the final result but cannot agree on the wording within the report. If they cannot be avoided, at least treat the dissenter(s) courteously and respectfully.

The method of presentation for the results should be a function of the decision-maker(s) preferences. (S)he may prefer a formal PowerPoint presentation, explanatory report, bulleted list, executive summary, or simple memo. This preference was determined early on by the savvy action officer. Some deciders may want full data dumps, others may prefer simple graphs and charts, and still others may just want a simple explanation. Remember that they suffer from information overload, so tell them what they need to tell their principal supporters or constituents. Generally, a formal report should be prepared and submitted, if not for review then at least for the file. Make sure you alert them to any lingering dissension or conflicts, especially if (s)he is a political appointee or elected official.

A memorandum to your boss is usually an acceptable format, though a draft memo to another boss may be appropriate. The idea is to submit a concise, self-contained document without additional comment. If your boss needs further information, (s)he will ask for it. The length of the briefing paper depends on the boss. My sub-cabinet boss insisted on only one page. President Barack Obama was willing to accept two or three pages, I am told.

A rough draft is perfectly fine and need not be a clean copy, but it must be complete and show a mature line of thought. It cannot be an attempt to shift the burden for staff work to your boss. If your boss returns it for rework, then you are guilty of incomplete staff work.

The final result should be a document that you would approve without reservation if you were the boss. You would stake your reputation on it.

*   *   *

Lesson #29: Prepare for a non-decision.

*   *   *

This implies that the decision-maker may defer a decision until later, for reasons which may or may not be apparent to you. For instance, I once had a director who would not make a major decision without sleeping on it, then would come into the office the next morning with a firm decision. Often, coordination with another official is necessary before a firm decision is made. Alternatively, an interim director may feel that any long-term decision is inappropriate until a permanent director is in place. It may therefore be a good idea to outline any benefits to waiting, even if an immediate decision seems more beneficial.

*   *   *

Lesson #30: Practice objections and prepare to overcome them.

*   *   *

You can predict what the decision-maker will object to and prepare a defense of your position. Try to put yourself in their position to predict what they will object to. You can also anticipate tough questions and prepare your answers. It may help to ask follow-up questions of the objector to better understand their concerns and obtain more information. Then go back to your office and fix your position to reflect their input.

* * *

Lesson #31: Leave yourself an out.

* * *

Resistance to change is due to management's lack of awareness or commitment, or else lack of money. So, convince them that change is necessary and beneficial. If that doesn't work, then use statistics to support the bottom-line cost benefits. Cost reduction opportunities often work best. Show management how change is better than the current condition. Anticipate the unexpected by taking proactive steps and face uncertainty head-on. Remember though that proper timing is crucial, so you may need to promote short-term success before pushing for the long-term. And naturally, your course of action must match the agency mission.

The desired end result is a commitment by the decision-maker to accept your solution (or a modification thereof) and closure. Providing a timeline is usually a good idea, unless the decision-maker is intransigent about timing, and shows that the other party will conserve time or cost through immediate implementation. And remember to be polite and follow up with the other party to ensure their satisfaction.

The ultimate decision must comply with current and future policies of the agency. One must take into account the impact on the rest of the agency. Public relations and marketing the solution to decision-makers and other offices within the agency may be required to assess their level of support or opposition and then to "sell the solution." This also means that political implications may enter the picture, since the agency has a political agenda in terms of implementing public policy.

It may be necessary to develop an implementation strategy. If so, consider all potential ramifications and prepare for their appearance and strategies to overcome them. The best way to do so is often brainstorming among team members, especially "out-of-the-box" ideas.

Maturity is necessary to overcome the human responses of frustration and overwhelming burden that results from changing priorities and requirements, as well as being overruled by higher management on an issue where the staffer feels strongly. The reasons for these changes and overrulings are not always communicated fully to the staffer. Further, multiple requirements require a juggling skill. And suspense dates must still be met. Hence, maturity plays a large role in successful staff work.

A good staffer can accept rejection of a recommendation, revise it, and resubmit it without a grudge or hurt feelings. A difference of opinion is not a personal attack by the decision-maker but does provide the staffer with a learning opportunity. Professional development is the end-result of good staff work, which provides the knowledge for future professional decision-making and the self-confidence needed for crisis management.

Chapter 9

Excellence on the Job:
Employee Dos and Don'ts

Ethics address professional actions in terms of behavior, character, conduct, and morality.[1] Executive Order 12674, "Principles of Ethical Conduct for Government Officers and Employees," April 12, 1989, as modified by Executive Order 12731 (same title), October 17, 1990, requires all public servants to:

- act without preferential treatment to any private organization or individual;
- avoid any actions creating the appearance of violating the law or ethical standards;[2]
- avoid financial transactions using government information for private interest;
- comply with all laws and regulations that provide equal opportunity for all Americans;
- disclose waste, fraud, abuse, and corruption to appropriate authorities;
- make no unauthorized commitments alleging to bind the government;
- place loyalty to the Constitution, law, and ethics above private gain;
- protect and conserve federal property;
- refrain from any financial interests or outside employment or activities that conflict with duty; and
- do not solicit or accept a gift or item of monetary value from any contractor or its employee.

Each agency head develops annual agency ethics training plans which include mandatory annual briefings on ethics and standards of conduct for all

---

1. Lindner, 50–51.
2. There is no allowance for a whistleblower to obtain part of any penalty imposed by a court, as would be the case in a *qui tam* action, where the claimant sues on behalf of both the government and self to assert a right or demand.

designated employees. Members of the senior executive service and military flag officers must file financial reports annually and face limits on outside income. All federal employees have current and post-employment restrictions on their financial interests and activities, which are subject to civil sanctions.

*　*　*

Lesson #32: Refrain from any outside activity that could create a conflict of interest.

*　*　*

All government employees must avoid conflicts of interest, namely personal or financial interests that conflict (or appear to conflict) with official responsibilities. For example, an individual cannot own stock in or show favoritism toward a company with which (s)he is dealing on the job. A classic example occurred with Darleen Druyan, who was the top civilian procurement official within the Air Force in the 1990s and who I had met once or twice. She had a reputation of being tough on contractors in her oversight and approval roles, and was never subject to any meaningful oversight because of this reputation. She was called the "dragon lady" by all I ever met who knew her.[3] However, about the year 2000, she sent the resumes of her daughter and her daughter's fiancé to Boeing, who hired them both. There was no law at the time to prevent this from happening. Two years later, though, she approved a plan to lease rather than buy a new generation of tanker aircraft from Boeing, then retired and took a job with the same company (which was illegal, both then and now) with a $250,000 salary plus a signing bonus (double what she made in the US Air Force). The DoD investigated Druyan and she admitted that she had inflated the prices and passed along information about a Boeing competitor. She spent nine months in jail. The two highest Boeing officials lost their jobs and the company was fined almost a billion dollars. Since there was no Air Force oversight of Druyan, this mess was not prevented, but should have been.

A friend of mine fell into the worst way this ethics policy can be enforced. He was tapped to become contracting officer for the largest procurement his agency had ever handled, the prize assignment of his career. Unfortunately, his supervisor learned that my friend's wife worked for a federal contractor whose sister division (not the one where she worked) might bid on the job. He was summarily withdrawn from the assignment merely because an appearance of impropriety could arise. There was no real conflict here, just some manager being overly cautious and thinking that maybe, perhaps, things would look shady. Fortunately, he survived this career setback and

---

3. A good article on this episode is Leung, "Cashing In for Profit?" CBS News.

eventually gained the top procurement spot in the agency and entered the Senior Executive Service.

Military officers also face ethics rules. Per 18 USC 281, retired regular military officers cannot ever sell anything to their former department, or else they will face a $10,000 fine and two years in prison.[4] 37 USC 801 prohibits the same officers from selling to anybody in DoD for the first three years of retirement. Since avoiding even the appearance of a conflict of interest is paramount, retired officers must complete a DD Form 1357 annually to address their activities. There is no criminal penalty for failure to furnish it, but it does contain an acknowledgement of the Privacy Act to avoid privacy concerns. Since this requirement is stated for all officers before they sign on, it is not considered to be discriminatory or a conflict of interest. This restriction does not apply to reserve officers to avoid concern over civilian job instability and insecurity, nor to active or reserve enlisted personnel.

Contractor employees undergo training each year to ensure that neither they nor their immediate family members have any financial interest or simultaneous employment with a subcontractor. Nor can they have any offer of prospective employment with another firm who might benefit from the knowledge they obtain during contract performance. Some contractors will go so far as to forbid their employees any financial benefit gained from any firm which does business with the federal government.

To avoid any conflict of interest or appearance of favoritism, no contractor owned or controlled by a government employee may receive an award.[5] This does not apply to special government employees (as defined in 18 USC 202) who serve as consultants or on advisory committees. However, the contract cannot arise directly out of the individual's activity as a special government employee, nor can the award be influenced by the special employee.

No federal employee may accept a bribe or gratuity. A *gratuity* is any item of monetary value given to an individual in expectation of receiving preferential treatment, and a *bribe* is a gratuity of money. The employee will be fired if this happens. I know of a quality assurance specialist who inspected and accepted a contractor's shipment, returned to his car, and found a 12-pack of beer in his trunk (prearranged, of course). He had no clue that the Naval Criminal Investigative Service was tipped off about his behavior and was watching him through binoculars. I hope he enjoyed his beer while searching for a new job!

Restrictions on individual behavior ensure integrity of the procurement process.[6] Procurement-sensitive information and contractor-specific information

---

4. *USC* stands for United States Code, which is the repository for all federal laws. The citation begins with the chapter number in the Code, followed by the section number, where the statute is recorded.

5. FAR 3.3 and Lindner, 57.

6. FAR 3.104.

cannot be released outside appropriate channels. An employee cannot use nonpublic information to advance one's own interest or a financial transaction. Also, no proposal or source-selection information may be disclosed before award by a government official (past or present) or advisor who had access to such information. Similarly, anybody who receives such information and does not report it is subject to criminal sanctions.

In accordance with the Procurement Integrity Act (41 USC 423), government employees cannot seek employment with potential outside hirers or contractors on a task where they are personally and substantially involved.[7] The term *participating personally and substantially* means to:

- develop or approve a solicitation, specification, or statement of work;
- evaluate offers;
- negotiate price or terms and conditions;
- recommend, review, or approve an award; or
- supervize an employee who performs any of these duties.

This definition excludes:

- certain general advisors;
- clerical support;
- members of boards or advisory committees who evaluate and recommend technologies or methods to achieve agency objectives; or
- participation in A-76 management studies.

Any government official engaged in a procurement action above the simplified acquisition threshold (currently $35,000) who is contacted by a hirer regarding possible employment must report the contact to a supervisor. The official must either reject the possibility of employment or else be disqualified from further involvement in the procurement action.

A one-year compensation ban applies to certain federal officials if the award value exceeded $10 million. These officials include:

- contracting officer;
- evaluator for either source selection or for financial or technical reasons;
- payment approver;
- program manager;
- rate determination official; or
- source selection authority.

---

7. FAR 104 and Lindner, 54–55.

However, this prohibition applies only to the division of the contractor performing under the given contract—the official is free to accept employment from the same corporation in a separate division or affiliate unrelated to this contract. Any violation of these laws could result in contract termination and contractor suspension or debarment. Damages are also possible.

Additional limitations apply to activities for any DoD official who leaves government service and participated personally and substantially in an acquisition over $10 million.[8] This applies to anyone who served as a:

- contracting officer;
- evaluation board member;
- flag officer;
- member of the Senior Executive Service;
- program manager or deputy; or
- source selection authority.

Such an official may not receive compensation from a DoD contractor for the first two years after leaving DoD service, unless first requesting a written opinion from a DoD ethics counselor regarding the applicability of post-employment restrictions. Nor can a DoD contractor knowingly provide compensation to such a covered DoD official within two years after leaving DoD service unless determining that the official has received or requested the post-employment ethics opinion at least 30 days beforehand. Failure to do so could lead to solicitation cancellation or contract termination, or even suspension or debarment.

DEPORTMENT AND APPEARANCE

Physical appearance and personal deportment can be critical for both employees and contractors, and the standards vary between offices. On-the-job behavior is critical to any office job and it is just as true in the federal government as in the private sector. In general, a stricter dress code is in force where senior managers are more demanding or the agency faces the public.

* * *

Lesson #33: Adjust your style and dress to the values of the agency.

* * *

---

8. DFARS 203.171.

My first day at a new client site was an eye-opener, as I saw every single male employee dressed in a suit (not merely blazer and tie) and every woman wore either a pantsuit or matching skirt and blazer ensemble. I had been working for the past 15 years in more relaxed dress code settings and only owned three suits at the time. That night, I asked my wife to accompany me to the nearby department store to expand my wardrobe!

*   *   *

Lesson #34: Learn how to manage your manager.

*   *   *

A new employee should determine at the outset what the boss considers important and is trying to accomplish. Conversely, find out what and who irritates the boss. I once worked with a very sweet young woman who was always frustrated because her boss (also female) only preferred employees who talked tough and projected a firm image with customers and colleagues alike. The young woman ultimately left for another office at a downgrade, thoroughly frustrated with our office, because she could not adjust to what her boss wanted and expected from the staff.

It is also important to learn how much the boss wants to confer with subordinates. I don't recall a single supervisor I ever had who did not want to confer with the rest of the team, but I hear that this does happen in some agencies. Hence, the new employee should identify to what extent the boss will accept input.

The employee must empathize with their boss and respect his/her needs. It is critical that the employee know how the boss reacts to stress. It is helpful to take on some burdens yourself, learn what upsets him/her and define problems ahead of time. Present issues as a heads-up before they become problems, and present one or more potential solutions to show you have thought them out thoroughly. Give the decision-maker time to decide—don't rush him/her. Show him/her how cooperation with your request will help achieve their goals. Remember to show loyalty and respect to the office employees and manager.

You must learn when to approach and when to leave alone, namely the best time to talk to him/her with a problem. I once had a division director who would occasionally blow his stack in a late morning meeting with any of his branch heads. Ten minutes later, he would ask the same person if he wanted to go to lunch. I could not understand the sudden change in this Jekyll-and-Hyde behavior, until one of the senior employees told me the secret to dealing with the director: "Take him to lunch, make sure he gets a full stomach, and after returning to the office you can get him to sign anything." The lesson here was learning how the manager behaved and planning accordingly.

There is an art form to saying "no" to your boss. First, acknowledge the importance of the issue, since it is already important to management. Then be unequivocal in saying no. Give reasons and offer alternatives. Also, you can offer to assist without getting involved in owning the problem, and maybe even declare your availability in your own time.

* * *

Lesson #35: Find a mentor immediately and network heavily.

* * *

A new employee should always strive to find a mentor in a new office, someone patient who can provide guidance when necessary and maintains a positive outlook. Get to know the power players—don't waste time with those who cannot help you. Networking is key, whether the office is large or small. This also means getting to know power players *outside* the office as well who can provide a different perspective to your career knowledge, and maybe even help you get a future job.

Another aspect of mentoring is to assess the political climate of the office and exploit it to your advantage, or even just to fit in. I once met a recent college graduate who worked for a very well-regarded agency. She quickly learned through the office grapevine that the best way to get face time with management was to join the office softball team. Although she did not pretend to be very athletic or coordinated, she realized that she had to attend practice and play when called, just to become known to management and promote a sense of social acceptance within the office.

* * *

Lesson #36: Learn from your mistakes and self-correct quickly.

* * *

A new employee should not be too afraid to trip up. You should always be willing to ask for help—nothing is more infuriating to a manager than someone who sits at their desk completely lost, staring at their computer screen and unable or unwilling to ask for help. It is a waste of time and salary to have such a nonproductive employee onboard. Besides, you cannot learn from your mistakes if you don't try. In my first job in Washington, D.C., my mentor said that our division director, whom I found quite intimidating at such an early point in my career, was nonetheless willing to tolerate any mistake—one time only. The idea was to learn from my mistakes and get it right the next time.

*   *   *

Lesson #37: Set high ethical and moral standards.

*   *   *

It is always best to create and promote a climate of pride and professional-ism. Do not show any fears or insecurity about the job. It is also a good idea to always share credit but not blame.

One should also maintain a positive attitude on the job. Don't grumble about work. Avoid criticizing the government or the agency, since news of dissatisfaction will surely get back to management. Do not utter any excuses or negatives or express anger. Instead, be nice to everyone in the office, even if someone is less than pleasant to you.

I had a colleague early in my career in Washington who constantly com-plained about the office, its management, and, especially, the city. He never hesitated to negatively compare Washington to his native Philadelphia or nearby Baltimore. Be it sports teams, public transportation, or the local popu-lation, his current place of employment came in last in his opinion. Worse, he complained about his managers behind their backs to colleagues, friends, and even contractors. It wasn't long before word got back to management. He never got a promotion, even though he could have received one without competition, and eventually left as an unhappy ex-employee.

*   *   *

Lesson #38: Keep your work area neat.

*   *   *

This lesson may surprise you. It is the first lesson I learned in my career. A sloppy office with papers strewn all over the desk and table sends a message of disorder to both co-workers and visitors. It is especially bad for a supervi-sor when the employees get such a message from an unkempt office. It is also important to place professional reading material in the workspace to project an image of professionalism. On one engagement where I spent only a day or two each week in the agency, I furnished my cubicle with several job-related books which I was not currently reading, just to remind the customer that I was technically competent.

*   *   *

Lesson #39: Plan your day's objectives and priorities.

*   *   *

Because organization is one of my strengths, I always planned the steps of the task at hand, prioritized them, and scheduled them in advance. This helped ensure that the task would be completed on time.

There are of course software products for prioritizing and time management, but a reminder: government offices provide employees desktops or laptops, so apps like Microsoft Calendar are pre-loaded. Similarly, government-furnished smartphones have pre-loaded software. In no case does the *user* have the legal authority or ability to download software onto such devices.

Early in my career, I worked with a colleague who was great fun to be around, but was not so well organized. As he obtained more challenging assignments, he began to fall behind in meeting his deadlines. This subject was brought up in his annual performance review and some brainstorming ensued to develop a solution. What he settled on was to list short-term and medium-term tasks on his chalkboard to form a "to-do" list. He highlighted urgent tasks that had to be done that day by marking a star in front of their listing. As he accomplished each task, he would cross it off the list. This not only prioritized his workload, but also provided a sense of accomplishment when he looked at the number of cross-offs. This was an excellent technique to help him accomplish his mission, and stood him well as he progressed in his career. He eventually became a department head within a DoD office.

* * *

Lesson #40: Avoid arrogance.

* * *

I once worked with a very arrogant man who rubbed everyone the wrong way. Among other duties, he worked up the annual preliminary budget and was therefore ruthless in challenging overhead expenses. But he wanted to enter the Senior Executive Service in the worst way, so he left his comfortable position in DoD to become a senior manager in a civilian agency. That did not last long. The change in employee priorities and behavior, coupled with his arrogance, made him the most hated man in the agency. Within a year, he was back in his old job in Defense. I met him again, years later, in his old position, just as arrogant and obnoxious as ever. Some people never learn, so it is best to accept them as is, deal with them as little as possible, and move on.

* * *

Lesson #41: Don't let the door hit you on the way out.

* * *

Another early lesson I heard from a Navy commander: If the boss makes a final decision, embrace it and execute it. You had your chance (hopefully) to express your opinion, but now it is time to do what you are told. If you cannot accept it, move on to another project (or even another job).

* * *

Lesson #42: Keep political and religious views to yourself. And keep your language clean.

* * *

There are some civil servants who are closet socialists and quite upset over how the government and politicians do things, even though they are working for the government. Others are ultra-conservative and don't get along with those of the first mindset. Then there are religious zealots who keep religious icons in their cubicle (to the fury of neutral managers) and get offended at anyone who speaks or acts offensively in the office. I have seen such people waste no time in running to management or Human Resources crying that the office is a *hostile work environment* as soon as a four-letter word or politically incorrect phrase is uttered in the vicinity of their cubicle. They are right of course, so all employees need to be especially careful of their opinions and language to avoid offending co-workers.

In this regard, we live in a society where swearing in public is becoming more common. Words which were previously bleeped out in television shows are now broadcast, and newspapers and blog sites routinely include such words in quotes or even in commentaries. Federal agencies have not yet adopted this practice as a matter of decorum. Enough civil servants still get upset over the use of profanity in the workplace that they consider it to be the sign of a hostile work environment. So it is best to refrain from its use in dealing with coworkers or over the telephone.

Maintain the attributes you expect to see in a successful employee:[9]

- be decisive and aggressive, but not so compliant as to be pushed around,
- be energetic and extroverted to contact and control people,
- develop a sense of humor,
- develop your own courses of action and make your own decisions,
- do not be content with mediocrity,
- do not procrastinate—do the distasteful part first,
- ignore those who preach anger, doom, or impossibility,
- maintain emotional stability and self-control of your reactions,

---

9. An excellent book I have found to address these attributes is Purves, *Secrets of Personal Command Power* (see Bibliography). It appears to be out of print, but is worth seeking out.

- maintain self-acceptance, self-confidence, and self-respect,
- never stop learning and growing,
- set goals—clear, vivid, and measurable,
- stay optimistic: do not get down when things go wrong,
- study successful people in the organization and follow their lead, and
- think and act like a winner.

*   *   *

Lesson #43: Act like you are privileged to work for the agency.

*   *   *

You may be the "new kid on the block" and need to fit in with those who have been employed for years in the same office. You will need to adopt their culture quickly to blend in. One should express pride in the agency you work for and share its values. Always see what you can do to help the office achieve its goals. This attitude will go miles in gaining acceptance and establishing your credibility within the office.

*   *   *

Lesson #44: Ask for advice and assistance from those who have already succeeded.

*   *   *

Early in my career, I was in a trainee position saddled with a weak manager who had a poor reputation and was just marking time to retirement. Since the work was seasonal in this office, during the off-season I read files of past work by the journeymen of the office. Then I went to them and asked questions such as "What does this mean?" and "Why did you do this?" No, tact was not a skill I had developed yet. Surprisingly, however, everybody answered my questions politely and cheerfully. Actually, a couple of them were stumped as to why they did what they did! They all appreciated that I was taking the time to learn from them, because they knew I wasn't learning from my boss. I scored points when it came to job rotation the next year and received a plum assignment, largely because of my self-initiative and willingness to learn.

*   *   *

Lesson #45: Build your value to the agency.

*   *   *

The more you accomplish, the greater management will value your performance and thereby increase your promotion ability. I built a reputation in my later years of coming into a consult in a pinch and resolving any outstanding issues. I became the "pinch-hitter" for the company and gained significant value in the eyes of management. I also collected information from a variety of sources not readily accessed by the office and fed it to management, thereby enhancing my value. Yes, it sometimes pays to listen to office gossip and pass it up the chain of command.

*   *   *

Lesson #46: Be mindful of your physical demeanor and body language.

*   *   *

Keep your posture erect. Stand upright rather than shifting around or walking stooped over. Use eye contact at all times. Maintain deep breathing from your back and abdominal muscles. This will force the emotion out of your voice and energy into it. End sentences with a lowered voice and overcome the "upspeak" style so common among some young persons (ending a sentence with a questioning tone), since it projects uncertainty in your voice.

A pet peeve of mine is talking with your hands. It distracts the other party from concentrating on what you say and instead leads them to watch the show being put on by your hand gestures. I have seen many people get sidetracked by watching hand puppet movements and lose the meaning of what the other person is saying. Don't do it.

*   *   *

Lesson #47: Deal in solutions—not problems.

*   *   *

Managers don't want to hear employees whine about yet another event that has gone wrong. Enough trouble has arisen in weekly events that you don't need to pour more fuel onto the fire. Instead, ensure that you have carefully thought out the problem and offer one or more solutions. And don't ever tell the boss what (s)he should do—this will only lead to another explosion in the office. Instead, work on providing helpful advice and solutions to the office to build your own value.

When I was running one of my contractor overhead studies, I was preparing a write-up on material overhead to type over the weekend and submit for review the following Monday. But on Thursday, I learned that we would have major findings due to inventory shortfalls in the contractor's storage room. There was no way I would have findings ready by Monday, much less a full report. So I told my management that I would substitute another portion of my team review, one that I was holding back because it was the easiest to write. This gave management something to read on time, accelerated a task I would have needed to do anyway, allowed my team to complete a thorough review in a serious problem area, and allowed me to save face. I found a solution to the problem.

* * *

Lesson #48: Learn from your boss.

* * *

All bosses have both good and bad points. Observe them in action, copy their strengths, identify their weaknesses, and develop ways to mitigate or overcome them. Every boss has developed some sense of business acumen or else they would not last in the job, so identify and incorporate their positive traits into your arsenal of successful techniques. Isolate their negative traits and qualities in your mind and don't adopt them—or even acknowledge them.

Getting to know your supervisor is absolutely essential to success. You will rely on this person to review and critique your work and guide you on the path to success.[10]

My very first boss in the federal government ran an office for simplified purchases. A number of purchase requests were urgently required for ship refit to ensure meeting deployment schedules. Every day, sailors would report to our office and walk through their requirements, then stand by my desk and wait while I placed the order and gave them the necessary paperwork. Often, they would then leave for their vans and pick up the material from a local vendor. My boss taught me the importance of responsiveness and customer satisfaction. When I was promoted to my next assignment, she said, "Dan, I didn't think you'd make it when you first came here. But you have really developed." Well, yes, in great part because of her patience in teaching me how to do the job and more importantly, what personal skills to develop.

* * *

Lesson #49: Get to work early and stay late.

* * *

Management will notice the early arrivals as go-getters and those who stay late as dedicated. Try to gain visibility. I also learned that an all-day meeting out of the office is not an invitation to change your commuting pattern for the day. Returning to the office after the meeting, even if only for a few minutes to check your e-mail, sends a positive signal to management.

---

10. An excellent work on this subject is *Managing Your Boss*, by Dorling Kindersley Publishing Staff. This book is very short—just 72 pages—but is a succinct, quick-reference book for tips on handling your supervisor. Another helpful work is an older title: *How to Manage Your Supervisor*, by Christopher Hegarty and Philip Goldberg.

I once took over chairmanship of a working group where my predecessor, admittedly not an "early bird," would not start the weekly status meeting until 9:30, and then let it drone on all morning long. The meeting brought in many people from other offices, so they had to drive over to our place and then back to their home offices. Since the meeting dragged everybody into lunchtime, many got back to the office in mid-afternoon, for perhaps only two hours of productive work that day. When I took over chairing the group, although I was unable to get all parties to move up the start time, I did insist on moving along and not bog down on side conversations. As a result, I succeeded in shortening the time length to 45 minutes. Kicking them out of the room at 10:15 was so far before lunch that they had no choice but to go straight back to the office, adding maybe three hours of productive time to their workday.

*   *   *

Lesson #50: Become friends with the administrative assistant.

*   *   *

The secretary or administrative assistant knows the ins and outs of the office and what works (and what doesn't). Cultivating a friendship can pay big dividends in terms of intangible benefits to the employee. Moreover, the secretary has the ear of the boss and can whisper a good word (or a negative one) to make or break the employee's reputation. Remember, a wise boss relies on the administrative assistant to be mindful of the tone of the office and what is happening outside the manager's office door.

*   *   *

Lesson #51: Persistence pays in getting results.

*   *   *

I once had a supervisory position where we obtained more and more work over time, which was a good thing because we were building value for the agency. Even with increased productivity, however, we were really scrambling to get it all done on time. Since much of the work was entry-level quality, I repeatedly asked for a trainee to come in and learn the business while helping to turn out work. Four formal requests later, I finally got a trainee. Persistence paid off, though it took several months to succeed.

*   *   *

Lesson #52: Set aside a moment each day for reflection.

*   *   *

I am not a big advocate of taking work home with you, and of course in a classified position this is nearly impossible. However, you can use time in the evening to decompress and recall the day's events. With the benefit of time and a restful home, and maybe a stiff drink, you can replay the circumstances to consider your options and decide the best course of action for tomorrow. I did this many times, always leading to a successful solution.

*   *   *

Lesson #53: Fight on-the-job boredom.

*   *   *

Inevitably, there are times when you lose focus on the job—let your mind wander or dread taking up a duty. But fight those feelings of boredom. An excellent way is to pursue a different task that is still job-related in order to change your focus and keep your mind sharp. Or take a short break. Stretch your legs. Get a second cup of coffee, tea, or water. Wandering around the office will at least give you some exercise, but be careful you don't enter a work area of a manager who resents visitors infringing on his territory (I did this once and, yes, I was called on the carpet for it).

Another way to get a break is to mingle with co-employees to talk about job-related issues. However, I would resist any discussion about last night's ballgame, lest another employee report you as "goofing off" on the clock. Since many offices have an employee who will bend your ear about the current pennant race or local team's playoff chances, you will need to tactfully defer this discussion to happy-hour time.

And resist the urge to get on social media (Twitter, Facebook, and the like). Keep it professional.

*   *   *

Lesson #54: Follow all of Murphy's Law.

*   *   *

"Murphy" actually propounded three laws and all are true, at least in my experience.[11] Nothing is as easy as it first seems because unforeseen complications arise. An interested party may unexpectedly show up with a concern to be resolved first. Second, every project I touched seemed to take four times longer than I originally thought because events are delayed, unforeseen developments occur, or input is late in arriving. Finally, if anything can go

---

11. There is disagreement on the origin of Murphy's Law. It cannot be authoritatively attributed to a smart man named Murphy, and it may originate in the 19th century or even earlier.

wrong, don't worry, it will. Then rework becomes necessary and further delay comes into play. Project plans and schedules must be revised to the right. And so on and so on. Speaking of projects . . .

*   *   *

Lesson #55: Learn how to get a project done.

*   *   *

This is actually very similar to staff work. Do your homework. Collect all the facts and related documents and e-mails. Develop an organized process to address the issue. Study the situation thoroughly and develop a solution. Then get agreement and support from your boss. You will need to develop a schedule and resources, using automated tools. Peer reviews help in adding expertise and achieving management buy-in. Then implement your project and follow-up with stakeholders. Any work product that is well researched and thought out will place the employee in a higher plane of respect among managers than one which is incomplete and poorly described.

*   *   *

Lesson #56: Surprise leads to panic leads to blame.

*   *   *

I once had a military boss on staff who seemed to get a surprise and urgent task every day. To get information and advice, he would then run around the office like his pants were on fire! Every unexpected development or task led to abject panic on his part. This behavior was not very conducive to team morale or mission achievement.

Don't let your boss ever get surprised on the job. You can never be sure if (s)he is having a bad day or has a hidden button. Instead, one should advise management as soon as trouble appears on the horizon. Moreover, don't let the boss get surprised in a meeting about something you knew or should have known. An embarrassed boss often leads to retribution against the employee who failed to issue an alert.

*   *   *

Lesson #57: Be careful what you ask for: you might get it.

*   *   *

You may not like the answer, or you might start a series of events that get quickly out of hand and lead to an undesired result. Make sure that you are capable of taking on a new challenge or task, or you will quickly get in over your head. Also make sure that the task has not left a trail littered with failure, or else you could merely add your name to that list.

Most often, I have seen this happen when someone aspires to a promotion, gets it, then discovers that the job was not what they expected or wanted. I have seen more than one person in this predicament, who either fails on the job or else takes a position in another office at the same pay level (known as a *lateral* move) to escape the problem job.

My employer once hired a young man just five years out of college to an operations position which would lead to becoming my supervisor. He reported to us very self-assured and declined any offers for help from his teammates. After 18 months, he asked to be reassigned to become a thought leader, a dead-end position in our company which limited his career growth in the company and led to a job search elsewhere. From my vantage point, he was afraid of face-to-face confrontations and felt very uncomfortable conducting annual performance appraisals. Once he got what he asked for, he wasn't very happy with it. He has since made a career as a thought leader with another company and staying on the forefront of technology, but not as a line supervisor.

* * *

Lesson #58: Be prepared and persistent.

* * *

Anticipating what might happen next is beneficial to any employee who works in an environment where dynamic recommendations and changes occur. Homework ahead of time is essential to your success and survival. Be persistent in researching and fleshing out potential actions and solutions.

An excellent and disappointing example of this occurred on one of my consultancies when the government representative suddenly announced one day that I should leave the contract because I had run out of work to do. This was actually true, so I had no objection or sense of disagreement with this decision. However, my project manager, who was new to the company, went further and told me to physically leave the office and return to our headquarters because my continued presence "might create an embarrassing scene." I had no idea what she meant by that comment, but I wasn't about to rock the boat because now I needed a new position. So I dutifully left and returned to the main office. Unknown to the project manager however, I had been with the company for several years and knew some people. Within 24 hours, three different vice-presidents reached out to me to offer assistance. When one of them offered me a firm position and I accepted, he asked why I had left the local office. He was incensed when I told him what the project manager had said. A few weeks later, when her mid-year performance appraisal went south, in part because of her decision to toss me out of the office, she made an appointment with Human Resources and abruptly resigned. She got what she wanted—my two-day departure—and more: her own permanent departure and a much-hurried job search.

* * *

Lesson #59: Learn all you can about your profession.

* * *

Since the government treasures expertise in its employees, the more you learn about your job content and career, the better. Study for any professional certifications you can; they will increase your competence and expertise and enhance your promotion potential. Pursue any training opportunities, especially if the agency will pay for it.

* * *

Lesson #60: Those who cannot learn from the past are doomed to repeat it.

* * *

It was George Santayana, a professor of philosophy and cultural critic at Harvard University, who first said something like this.[12] This lesson reflects the action I mentioned before about reading files of past actions and learning from other people's actions and mistakes. Most offices have archives of past actions on the same subject or similar activities. Find them, read them, and learn from them. Do the successful actions as before and don't repeat past mistakes.

* * *

Lesson #61: Volunteer.

* * *

Serving on a committee or special assignment is a great way for a junior employee to gain the attention of management. It helps lead to promotions, too. In my experience, however, this approach does not often pay dividends for a journeyman wishing to move up to a managerial position. However, someone in the operational field can participate on a professional committee and gain a staff position by appealing to other staffers serving on the same committee. A similar approach is to attend and participate in meetings and volunteer positions of a professional society.

---

12. Santayana, *Reason in Common Sense*, 284.

Another key to success in a government job is to learn the art of conversation.[13]

* * *

Lesson #62: Use business-savvy communication skills.

* * *

Listening is critical to successful communication. You must filter out biases and emotions, use people's names, don't interrupt, ask questions to test your interpretation, and be sensitive to their feelings. Being nonjudgmental is important to avoid offending the other person and show that you are truly interested in what they say. Good ways of doing this include saying:

- I hope you understand,
- I'll do it right away,
- I'll get back to you,
- I'm sorry,
- It seems,
- It's possible,
- Let me explain,
- Let's review together, and
- We can try this.

The wrong ways to communicate include such phrases as:

- I don't know,
- You should, ought, or must,
- You know, or
- You're wrong.

* * *

Lesson #63: Develop good negotiating skills.

* * *

Negotiating is a critical element of success in any government position, as you will continuously deal with persons of different interests or different constituencies.[14] Hence,

---

13. An excellent resource is *Smart Talk: The Art of Savvy Business Conversation*, by Roberta Roesch.

14. The classic book on this subject is *Fundamentals of Negotiating*, by Gerard I. Nierenberg.

- anticipate questions and develop answers;
- concentrate on content, not person or method;
- cost out every concession before making it;
- determine your and their needs and wants;
- don't answer a question until you understand it;
- don't criticize in public;
- don't interrupt;
- find common areas of interest and interdependencies;
- first get understandings, then agreements in principle, then firm agreements;
- get all their demands on the table before starting and then restate your demands;
- get something in return for every concession;
- get them to concede first on major issues;
- keep calm and collected, don't lose your cool;
- keep notes of what happens;
- provide room to maneuver;
- put burden of proof on other side;
- restate the other side's position clearly;
- set time limits on offers and get a firm answer;
- show sympathy and understanding;
- start with areas of easy agreement;
- think before you speak; and
- track progress toward goals.

TO CONCLUDE

The most memorable source I have found for clever sayings about on-the-job performance is from Norman Augustine, former president of Martin Marietta Corporation. Here are some of my favorite quotations from him and others:[15]

- "The last ten percent of performance generates one-third of the cost and two-thirds of the problem." —Norman Augustine
- "When all else fails, read the instructions." —"Murphy"
- "A revised schedule is to a business what a new season is to an athlete or a new canvas to an artist." —Norman Augustine
- "When the going gets tough, everyone leaves." —Lynch's Law
- "The optimum committee has no members." —Norman Augustine
- "When in doubt, suggest a committee be appointed." —Harry Chapman

---

15. Augustine, *Augustine's Laws.*

- "Fool me once, shame on you. Fool me twice, shame on me." —Native American proverb
- "You gotta have rules, but you also gotta allow for a fella to mess up once in a while." —Bum Phillips
- "Law is like sausage. If you like it, you shouldn't watch it being made." —Otto von Bismarck

Chapter 10

Managing—Supervision

Good management begins at the very top of an agency, with proper strategic management and planning. *Strategic planning* plays a key role in federal operations. This is a structured methodology to make decisions and take actions to guide the agency toward fulfilling its mission. This involves those concepts, procedures, and tools to help decision-makers decide what is important to reach their goals in all time frames: short, intermediate, and long terms. Although strategic planning was always part of federal practice, it has been brought into sharper focus due to the Government Performance and Results Act of 1993 and the Government Performance and Results Modernization Act of 2010.[1] To some extent, strategic planning has resulted in a greater emphasis on customer service, outcomes, or results, and discretion in achieving same. There is a tendency in some agencies to become less bureaucratic and furnish greater discretion to managers.

Careful thought is necessary upfront when introducing strategic planning to an agency. Purposes and goals must be delineated in terms of administrative, ethical, legal, and political environments. Usually, a broad agenda must first be established before specific actions can be considered. Decision-makers and stakeholders must be identified and their interests properly considered. Input is often necessary from both lateral and vertical strata within the agency. Both near-term and long-term consequences must be reflected in strategic thinking. In classic risk management terms, a *SWOT analysis* must be performed to identify the (S)strengths, (W)weaknesses, (O)opportunities, and (T)threats to the organization. Implementation plans must be realistic and achievable, and flexibility in both goal setting and implementation is often essential.

---

1. 31 USC 1115 and 31 USC 1101, respectively.

The basic methodology of strategic planning within the federal government is what political scientists call the Harvard Policy Model (originally formulated in the 1920s), or at least a derivative thereof. This process seeks to tie together a business unit and its environment through the SWOT analysis, management values, and agency social obligations.[2] It practices *portfolio management* for a collection of programs and budgets (and conceivably, agencies) which includes consideration of at least the following:

- stakeholders, especially when hierarchy or shared power is not apparent within the agency;
- organizational goals, mission, and values;
- upcoming challenges and changes to analyze future issues;
- strategies to address these issues;
- implementation plans, updated as information arrives and situations evolve; and
- continuous reevaluation.

The practice of portfolio management has gained wide acceptance in the past 20 years because offices often have multiple projects to manage at one time. Although portfolio management provides insight into the various components of an organization, it is often difficult to identify their dimensions, fit each component into a comprehensive planning process, and manage those programs that wind up "losing" in the competition for management attention and resources.

Because power and politics constantly change and relationships therefore change, incremental change is often necessary. However, care must be taken not to lose sight of agency mission or innovation by focusing on control. In fact, losing track of strategic issues is a major danger to strategic planning. Innovation is also critical to successful strategic management. It is also critical to supervision of federal employees.

The art of supervision involves enabling and motivating subordinates or team members to meet agency goals. The supervisor creates an environment conducive to reaching these goals, simplifying complex problems to achievable tasks and relating to the needs and wants of team members. Improvement of their on-the-job skills should be paramount in a supervisor's mind, especially for the sake of employee accountability. There are literally thousands of books and publications dealing with this issue—pick one, or several, as your guide.

Behavioral management training courses will often begin with the scientific management style developed by Frederick Winslow Taylor in the influ-

---

2. Bower et al., *Business Policy.*

ential book *The Principles of Scientific Management* (1911).[3] This approach expresses employee motivation in economic terms, where financial rewards such as pay raises and bonuses are the best method to improve employee performance. Of course, personal satisfaction and a sense of accomplishment may also come into play for an individual employee. Nonetheless, annual bonuses are common for stellar performance in the federal government, and non-competitive promotions for lower-grade employees are frequent. Hence, Taylor's approach to scientific management still has some applicability in the federal environment.

It is useful for a supervisor to understand the theory first propounded in 1960 by Douglas McGregor, a professor of management at the Sloan School of Management, Massachusetts Institute of Technology.[4] McGregor argued that how a manager makes assumptions about individual behavior and nature will influence his/her management style toward employees. McGregor created two contrasting approaches to management style, which he labeled "Theory X" and "Theory Y." The Theory X manager was old school and believed that employees were indifferent and unmotivated, and largely resistant to change. Managers of these employees must furnish strong leadership and motivation, sometimes exercising punitive controls to obtain results. In contrast, Theory Y managers believe their employees are highly creative and motivated to succeed in meeting both agency goals and their own desire for achievement. These managers encourage employee participation in setting and achieving goals, working together in teams to solve problems, and participating in decision-making.

A few managers today are still classic Theory X autocrats, making decisions without regard to their employees or concern about the impact on them. Communication is often one-way, top-down, and morale is often quite low. Some practice a traditional transactional style where employee compliance with management is based on a prescribed system of rewards and punishments, often couched as incentives, which may be efficient but could produce mediocre results.

The opposite (Theory Y) style is democratic, where employees have input in decision-making and communication is a two-way street. However, decision-making is often slowed down in this manner. An alternative is a hands-off approach where the employees are let loose to do their jobs at their own pace using their own style. Often used in a research environment, these employees may thrive in such an approach; however, there may be limited oversight and little or no chance for corrective action to be taken.

---

3. Drury, "Scientific Management: A History and Criticism," *Studies in History, Economics and Public Law*.

4. McGregor, *The Human Side of Enterprise*.

Theory X is not common anymore because work roles are becoming more specialized. Managers do not need to spend so much time instructing employees on tasks and monitoring their performance, freeing the manager to spend more time on his/her own work. Moreover, turnover is reduced as employees feel empowered over their work accomplishment and career success. Moreover, the Theory Y management style encourages employees to participate in discussions and contribute to the good of the agency. They are also encouraged to engage with colleagues to build teamwork and unity. This will lead to increased productivity and accountability of each employee.

                              *   *   *

Lesson #64: A good leader will strive to improve the performance of all.

                              *   *   *

This approach will lead employees to feel self-worth, a strong desire to contribute, and greater certainty of their own talents and abilities. The leader should show them how to approach problems so they will solve them next time. Employees want to know how they are doing and what is expected of them. This approach will also eliminate boredom, use positive feedback not criticism, and instill a desire to work hard and seek out difficult and challenging tasks. The wise leader will determine the required results, create plans to achieve them, and develop relevant measures of performance for both employee feedback and management reports. Of course, actions must match their words.

There is a difference between being a leader and being a manager. Management is what you do, whereas leadership is how you think. I have encountered a few people who manage based on skills they learned in their studies for a Masters' degree in Business Administration, but they are so focused on process that they never learn how to lead, with the results of missed deadlines and unfulfilled programs. Both sets of skills—leading and managing—are necessary in today's managers. After all, it's not what you know, it's what you do with what you know that counts.

TEAMS

So much work in the federal government is done in a team environment that this topic deserves further discussion. Teams are useful in gathering different perspectives to performing tasks and solving problems, which tends to enhance critical thinking within the agency. Because of its very nature, team building is often used to revise and broadcast work objectives, and with setting and meeting goals. Team members provide input to defining success and failure to reach agency goals, thereby buying in to the agency mission and gaining ownership of the solution. This is a major benefit to improving processes within the agency. Teamwork also builds employee motivation and builds effective relationships with coworkers.

There is no set limit on team size. I have seen teams numbering in the mid-teens work effectively. Larger teams certainly bring a wider variety of experiences and abilities to the table. I have also run a team of four, and even two, members which worked just fine. It all depends on the complexity of the project and how many sources of expertise and representation are necessary and appropriate.

There are challenges to team building. Employees must be team-oriented; those who are individualists will not respond to a group dynamic. Cross-functional and cross-agency team members may bring different work cultures, ethics, and values which do not mesh. Of course, the "not-invented-here" attitude pervades several offices who insist on protecting their turf and will not compromise their positions and approaches for the sake of a team. Further, the proliferation of remote workers and telecommuters will deny face-to-face contacts unless videoconferencing is implemented. Roles and responsibilities of each team member must be clearly understood by all team members and leaders to avoid confusion and ensure that all bases are covered.

If there are multiple team leaders, they absolutely must work together and make decisions jointly rather than separately. This way, the team will only be pulled in one direction. To accomplish this, the norm is for the team leader who consumes the largest block of the employee's time to take the lead in the employee's time management and performance appraisal. Of course, good communication skills among the leaders is a must for this approach to work. This is especially true if flexibility to a changing environment is involved.

Team building stresses both the various roles of individuals and social relations among individuals. It is used to ensure alignment around agency goals (including defining success and failure to meet goals), building effective relationships among employees, and solving team or shared problems (such as communication and sharing). Increased communication leads to conflict resolution, interdependence, job satisfaction, and shared accountability and responsibility. Other benefits often include boundary setting, cooperation on work tasks, mutual trust, and risk-taking.

*   *   *

Lesson #65: A wise manager protects his or her teammates.

*   *   *

One of my division directors made it his job to go to command meetings and return with any tasks assigned by higher management. Then he would research the issue himself and develop a response, properly vetted through the branch heads. He deliberately did not involve the rank-and-file employees because he wanted to insulate them from these external interruptions, which he often viewed as "busy work" that would distract us from our daily operational duties. When he did need input from us, he would sheepishly knock on our door and apologetically ask for the necessary information. He was very protective of our time and shielded us from the distractions imposed by higher command.

* * *

Lesson #66: Be a team player.

* * *

I had a situation once when we learned at 4:00 PM that we had to present a great deal of information at a quickly arranged meeting first thing next morning. I only had one other teammate, so we were hustling to collect, collate, and copy the data we needed. Our next door neighbor, who worked for our company but was not on our team, dropped everything he was doing and pitched in to help, without asking. We got everything done within an hour and got a good night's rest, largely thanks to this other employee being a good team player. The next morning, on my way to work, I texted our project manager on how helpful this fellow had been in volunteering to help. He got an "atta boy" from our project manager. This episode also proves another rule:

* * *

Lesson #67: Find a reason to compliment fellow team players to management.

* * *

There are several organic problems which the process of team management could create. Employees could fear confrontation with their boss and lose trust in each other. Resultant failure to express their opinions could lead to lack of commitment on the part of the employees, as well as a lack of accountability toward each other. They may not feel responsibility for failure to perform or achieve agency goals. Some employees will take advantage of the opportunity to slack off on the job and push responsibility onto others. Supervisors who fear confrontation may also refrain from holding employees responsible for their actions. Common solutions to these problems include team members asking each other for help and advice, and two-way feedback during annual performance appraisals.

There can be several benefits to teamwork:

- building relationships and reducing conflict among team members,
- common performance standards,
- improved performance and productivity,
- motivation through increased productivity and peer competition, and
- problem solving by bringing together persons with different skill sets and experiences.

* * *

Lesson #68: Be a champion of the cause.

* * *

Champions are needed within the agency to manage the daily process and any organizational transformations to ensure employee buy-in and motivation, as well as information feedback. Today's manager must openly advocate written, verbal, and non-verbal communication, and should invite continuous and transparent discussion for employees to provide opinions and suggestions. Doing so encourages employee participation as well as commitment and loyalty, shared values, and organizational identity.

The best and most famous example of championship I encountered was in the program office that managed construction of the Polaris missile. This office was created in 1955 during the height of the Cold War, when the Navy decided to build an intercontinental ballistic missile that could be ejected from a stealth submarine, break the surface of the ocean, fly through the atmosphere, and hit a target with pinpoint precision 1,500 miles away. This concept was beyond the state of the art at the time—there was no submarine in existence at that time that could house and fire such a missile. But the commanding officer, Rear (later Vice) Admiral William "Red" Raborn, took hold of the technological and managerial challenges, creating the Program Evaluation and Review Technique (PERT)[5] that is commonly used today and covered in every college course on business management. He was given eight years to accomplish this amazing task, and incredibly achieved it in just five years. He championed the cause and succeeded beyond the Navy's wildest dreams.

* * *

Lesson #69: Motivate your team members.

* * *

---

5. There is an excellent chapter on PERT in Meredith et al., *Project Management in Practice.*

Motivation goes hand-in-hand with championing. Self-motivation is critical to success. You can't get anything done unless you get people to do it. You will need to explain both the work assignment and your expectations in achieving it. Allow the team member to ask questions, be sure (s)he understands, and show him or her your trust and support. Moreover, the way you treat your team members is just as important:

- ask how (s)he can improve his or her work so you will learn reasons for any bad work habits;
- ask open-ended questions such as "What do you want to accomplish next?" and "How can I help?";
- build rapport by finding common ground, be it children or sports or mission;
- don't say certainly or undoubtedly if your position is disputable—instead say "it appears" or "if I'm not mistaken";
- never argue or lecture, but rather work out a positive and agreeable course of action;
- provide constructive feedback and praise;
- remain open to alternative ways to solve the problem;
- smile and personalize your e-mails, such as "I hope you enjoyed your weekend";
- understand the other person's interests and concerns;
- when giving feedback, talk about actions and results, not the person; and
- when receiving feedback, ask questions to clarify.

GENERAL MANAGERIAL ADVICE

*   *   *

Lesson #70: Recognize and overcome your flaws.

*   *   *

Continuously examine yourself to learn from your mistakes and improve yourself. Maintain a positive outlook that you will overcome your flaw and challenges with confidence. Anticipate problems likely to arise and how to avoid them. Learn to analyze a situation and problems and people, and develop methods to overcome any barriers, including your own. As I previously mentioned, in my first job, I recognized my lack of organizational and personal skills and worked to resolve them so I could succeed.

*   *   *

Lesson #71: Don't be too casual on the job.

*   *   *

Office workers look to the manager to set the tone for the office. If the manager is lackadaisical or too informal, the subordinates will take the cue and adopt the same behavior. Work quality will suffer, deadlines may be missed, and ultimately morale will suffer. Instead, the manager must set a professional tone for the office and pursue deadlines and quality with an appropriate amount of professionalism and zeal. I once saw a manager hired from outside our office to take over a weak branch (not mine, thankfully) and replace a very laidback supervisor who was largely "retired on the job." The new manager whipped his people into shape, several of whom were new hires and had picked up some bad habits from his predecessor. They improved in a short time as a result of his professionalism and removal of casualness.

*   *   *

Lesson #72: Don't assume.

*   *   *

Just look at the word "assume" and split it into three words, of three ("*ss"), one ("u"), and two letters ("me"), respectively, to get "To assume makes an *ss out of you and me." You will see what a mistake it is to believe you know the facts without really knowing them. It is imperative that you have all the facts and necessary input before jumping to conclusions.

This was one of the first lessons I learned in my career. I was involved in planning a goodwill tour of warships to the Great Lakes to "fly the flag" in that part of the country. We needed to hire local pilots at two different choke points on the journey. I contacted the first one and learned what information he needed about the vessel he would guide in order to quote his price. Naively, I proceeded to try and fit this model to the other pilot. Fortunately, my boss correctly told me to contact the other pilot first to see how he put his pricing model together. You guessed it—the pilots used different inputs in their models. For instance, one was concerned about the vessel's draft (depth of the hull below the water line), while the other focused on beam (width) and couldn't care less about draft. And so on. Lesson learned: do a thorough job of fact-finding and don't make assumptions about how others may think.

*   *   *

Lesson #73: Conflict is inevitable: learn how to manage it.

*   *   *

Conflict is caused by poor communications and by different perceptions, values, or preferred solutions. To overcome conflict, one must review the facts, often presenting more information, and identify the higher ideals held by all people to justify any necessary compromise. You should acquiesce if you realize you are wrong or the issue is more important than winning. Remember that often, the relationship is more important than the conflict. You can change behaviors but not people.

A critical role I once filled was chairing a technical panel of members from the various armed services. One service was particularly difficult to work with because they did not trust solutions born outside of their service and had their own unique way of doing things. It took a lot of patience to defuse the conflicting positions and a great deal of hand-holding to get them to agree with what we wanted for the rest of DoD. Sometimes we went along with their position because it made sense and could integrate with what the rest of DoD did. Ultimately, I got unanimous agreement on what to do and how to do it.

Another time while in the same job, I needed two separate teams to work together and develop a common position that all could agree to. Good luck with that! So I asked my military aide, an Air Force captain, to keep an eye on them. She intuitively replied, "Oh, you mean provide some adult supervision?" Yes, I did mean that.[6]

*   *   *

Lesson #74: The best learning ground for management is . . . parenthood. Think like a parent.

*   *   *

Sometimes, getting all these people on the same page is like herding cats. They come to the table with different objectives, different agendas, and different orders from their home offices. Nonetheless, the manager is responsible for facilitating deliberations to craft a solution for all (or at least most) stakeholders. Of course, if the manager has ultimate authority to make a decision, the task becomes somewhat easier. Even in this case, however, the manager must try to get buy-in from all stakeholders to avoid future resis-

---

6. I was pleased to hear that she was selected for promotion shortly after this episode. Undoubtedly due to possessing this important managerial skill! Ironically, she left the Air Force some time thereafter—to become the full-time mother of twins!

tance. It becomes necessary to gently guide them toward a common solution. This is not unlike getting children ready to leave the house on a family outing or working together on a school project.

* * *

Lesson #75: Facts are power.

* * *

Numbers synthesize the effects of many individual items. They often are tinged with assumptions and people's thoughts. Moreover, they can be manipulated by the speaker to whatever end is desired. Hence, a wise manager will get the facts from several sources. The manager must ask questions and do homework, and often run some quantitative analytics, to understand what is being encountered.

* * *

Lesson #76: Learn how to make rational decisions.

* * *

There are several definite steps in the decision-making process:

• define the problem,
• establish objectives,
• collect facts,
• evaluate the effectiveness of each alternatives,
• assess potential negative consequences of each alternative,
• select the best alternative,
• monitor progress, and
• correct deviations.

Planning is so important in federal operations because the work is often predictable, at least in most offices. Hence,

* * *

Lesson #77: If you fail to plan, you plan to fail.

* * *

A military way to say this is, "Plan ahead for the next war." If the problem cannot be resolved, then you will need to manage it, not ignore it. As Admiral Grace Hopper, the mother of computer usage within the Navy and the first woman to make admiral said, "Go ahead and do it—you can always apologize later."[7] I have occasionally (though fortunately, rarely) consciously made decisions that I knew would get criticized later (and they did), but I went ahead and executed them on-the-spot to accomplish the mission in a timely manner. Though unpleasant, the criticism was from an outside source and a small price to pay for meeting our goals. I followed Admiral Hopper's advice and took my medicine later—after I had achieved our objective. No negative repercussions occurred.

*   *   *

Lesson #78: Don't ask the question if you don't want to hear the answer.

*   *   *

A manager must be willing to accept bad news. Sometimes, this seems to happen on a daily basis! Nonetheless, it is necessary to find out what is going wrong as well as right because it can head off problems. Besides, you might learn some things you did not know but were afraid to ask about.

You must sometimes question things to move forward: "Why are we doing this? Why are we doing it *this* way?" I once worked on an efficiency study for a storage and refit facility in which I was appalled to see sailors playing cards while on duty. They literally had nothing to do because they had no vessels in port to load. The study recommended that the services be contracted out, resulting in the elimination of 26 unnecessary military billets. My manager not only embraced this approach, but wondered out loud why we couldn't do this at other refit facilities. We showed him something that was going wrong, and he not only embraced our news but also applied the lessons learned to other facilities in the fleet.

A manager must therefore be receptive to new ideas and find creative people. Be sensitive to others and accept them for what they are, because they probably won't change.

*   *   *

Lesson #79: Focus on the important issues.

*   *   *

Do not waste time on insignificant aspects of the problem. Senior managers learn to do this just to survive. They can get easily bogged down in minutiae and lose track of "the big picture." I knew a senior executive who was very detail-oriented throughout his career and could not break himself

---

7. *The New York Times*, August 14, 1986, B6.

of the habit as he advanced. Even as an executive, he would slow down approval processes, delay meetings while people waited for him, and never leave before 6 PM at night. He was not universally loved, to say the least, not because he was nasty (he was actually very pleasant to talk to) but because he was slow to approve and even slower to deal with human relations issues. It is essential for managers to keep focused on the end goal and critical issues at hand. In a related vein,

* * *

Lesson #80: Confront a crisis before it becomes a catastrophe.

* * *

It does no good to delay the inevitable when trouble arises. Never. The crisis will only get worse. It is better to address the issue immediately and develop an action plan to resolve it. Submit requests for any necessary resources promptly and round up any personnel useful to work the issue.

I began a consult with FEMA one year after Hurricane Katrina hit the United States in August 2005. Their procurement process was troubled with extensive delays and missing requisitions. As a result, important support equipment and contract services were not being awarded. Moreover, with the end of the fiscal year approaching, FEMA would not receive an extension on the life of the money, since they are funded on a quarterly basis. This meant that the money would soon be gone, and with it any chance of making these purchases. With this crisis staring us in the face, I began to track down dozens of missing procurement requests and work closely with the procurement office to follow the status of those requests they had received. Over time, my program manager obtained two other persons to help me out in the tracking process. We were finally able to track down and award 100 percent of all procurement requests. A catastrophe was averted because we addressed the crisis quickly and head-on at the outset.

* * *

Lesson #81: Look for common ground.

* * *

This was the campaign mantra of Jesse Jackson when he ran for president in 1988. A manager must build consensus in many issues because different people bring different perspectives. It is necessary to find common ground to ensure that all stakeholders buy into the decision, as well as all employees and teammates. This requires tenacity and the ability to meld disparate opinions into a cohesive position satisfactory to all (or at least most) of the parties affected. This was the secret to my success in chairing multiservice working groups and drafting requirements to be applied throughout DoD.

Unfortunately, the well-known Peter Principle applies all too often in the federal government:[8]

*   *   *

Lesson #82: Some employees rise to their level of incompetence.

*   *   *

The corollary of this statement is: "Work is accomplished by those employees who have not yet risen to their level of incompetence." I once worked with a bright young man, a real go-getter, hard worker—until he became a supervisor. Then he pushed all the work off on his team, spent all his time schmoozing with higher-ups, and didn't help his team members to succeed. Needless to say, this did not engender goodwill with his teammates. His career did not take off and he did not achieve the high-level position to which he aspired.

I worked with a civilian who did a splendid job as a deputy program manager, working under a military officer. When the officer decided to retire early due to a health scare, the civilian was the logical choice to replace him, and eagerly agreed to do so. Problems quickly developed with contractor performance and government requirements, resulting in missed deliveries and concerns about quality. When an aggressive new general took over the command, he literally fired the civilian on his first day on the job, transferring him to a sterile desk job to complete his career. The civilian got what he asked for—his own program—and lived to regret it.

*   *   *

Lesson #83: Change is our friend.

*   *   *

This rule is a direct quote from a Navy captain I once worked for. Time marches on and developments cause us to revise our priorities. Some tasks disappear, new ones appear, and work methods evolve. Since so many civil servants are averse to change, it is essential for the leader to embrace change for the opportunities it brings. I must say, this is one area where federal managers have improved over time. Today's managers that I have seen are more willing to break down barriers, try new things, and promote change within their agency than their predecessors did.

---

8. Peter and Hull, *The Peter Principle*.

The best book I ever found on management style is *Leadership Secrets of Attila the Hun* by Wess Roberts.[9] Some of his secrets apply very nicely to federal work:

- Anticipate other people's actions, characteristics, motives, priorities, thoughts, and values
- Apply common sense to solve complex problems
- Be willing to learn, listen, and grow in awareness and your abilities to perform duties
- By actions—not words—you establish integrity and morale
- Don't blame the guiltless
- Don't decide when you don't understand
- Don't expect everyone to agree with you
- Don't expect to change long-term traditions
- Don't delegate and then try to manage the issue—your subordinate will not be happy
- Encourage creativity, freedom of action, and innovation among subordinates
- Express gratitude for those who serve you well
- Feel free to disagree but don't discourage
- Focus on opportunities rather than problems
- Give a subordinate appropriate challenges at successively higher levels of responsibility
- A healthy body supports a healthy mind
- Leadership success depends on preparation, experience, and opportunity
- Learn more from failure than from success
- Learn to deal with adversity and overcome mistakes
- Listen to both the good and bad news
- Perception is reality
- Persistence in the face of challenge and opportunity is necessary
- Recover from disappointment without losing perspective
- Resolve to do the right thing
- Show concern for your employees and their families
- Superficial goals lead to superficial results
- Those above and below you count on your leadership ability—be proud of it.

9. Roberts, *Leadership Secrets of Attila the Hun.*

Chapter 11

Communication

I have found that the biggest problem both employee and supervisor face in the federal government is inadequate communication, both top-to-bottom and the opposite, as well as laterally between offices. *Organizational communication* is the process of sharing information about its activities in order to advance and achieve its goals. It includes vertical channels such as top-to-bottom from upper management to employees, or bottom-to-top through beneficial suggestion programs and similar feedback. It can also be horizontal through employee interest groups, internal e-mails, or personal discussions. These communications can be formal or informal, oral or written, internal or external.

Internal communications are often essential to provide information and feedback of organizational initiatives, mission and vision, performance, and policies. Official paths of communications work on a traditional top-to-bottom scalar approach and include organizational memos, newsletters, and policy directives. These paths tend to focus solely on managerial priorities without the emotional or social benefits sought by employees. However, you never know where you may pick up information beneficial to you and your job performance.

* * *

Lesson #84: Maintain informal channels of communication.

* * *

Unofficial networks include the proverbial grapevine and gossip sources such as e-mail and the coffee mess, social media, and after-hours happy hours and telephone calls. These may seem authentic because they are more personal than the cold official statements issued by management and vetted by legal

counsel. However, informal communications can be misleading if not dangerous because they may be emotional, opinionated, full of rumor, and totally
incorrect. Hence, two-way (or even every-way) communication is essential to
provide continuous and effective feedback so that the organization continues to
succeed and the employees develop trust in their management. However,

*   *   *

Lesson #85: Take any informal communications with a grain of salt.

*   *   *

Face-to-face communications is still the preferred means of communications. Visual cues can reinforce what is said and reveal hidden problems or
misconceptions, as well as discuss any conflicts or crises. It also promotes
among the employees a sense that their boss is available for help and consul-
tation, rather than hiding behind an office door or not caring about employees' well-being.

Both formal and informal methods must promote feedback to assess control and desirable changes. This is critical to the federal government, which
tends to be a series of closed systems which are inherently resistant to change
and any open communications with the outside world, at least the world
beyond its constituency and environment. For instance, the Department of
Agriculture employees will pay close attention to farmers' feedback and the
food industry, but perhaps not as much to urbanites.

It appears axiomatic that corporate communication reinforces its culture
through informal channels and social activities. Corporate culture reinforces
communications by using agency vocabulary and shared practices. Culture of
an agency marks its identity and includes its:

- behaviors and work rules,
- hierarchies,
- level of customer focus,
- policies,
- socialization methods, and
- values and beliefs.

*   *   *

Lesson #86: Share important information with teammates.

*   *   *

The team leader should use collaboration software and e-mail to communicate with team members daily. S(he) should solicit regular feedback from
team members to get agreement on where the team is going.

You might ask whether it is good to keep an open-door policy or keep the door closed. I have done both in my career and found that it all depends on the manager's workload, not the other team members. Yes, supervisors have plenty of their own work to do, and when it needs to be done, interruptions need to be kept to a minimum. That means, close the door. On those days with a light workload and you are in an approachable spirit, then by all means keep it open to encourage team members to consult with you. This should be a personal decision by the manager based on working conditions and workload.

* * *

Lesson #87: Return phone calls and e-mails.

* * *

It is rude to ignore messages asking for help or useful information. Requests for action should be promptly answered. If you are not the proper individual to address the issue, indicate who is. Even if the message is just to provide a tidbit of information, send a response e-mail thanking the sender, even if you did not ask for the information. And most certainly respond if you did ask for the input.

* * *

Lesson #88: Minimize your words.

* * *

Speak clearly and directly in a professional setting. Rambling on is a real turnoff and loses the attention of the other person. It is often wise to practice what you will say beforehand. E-mail offers an excellent opportunity to do this because you can proofread your words and revise whenever a different interpretation or thought occurs. You must also think about what the recipient party will think and respond. I often spend half an hour composing an e-mail message because I would imagine what the other party might think and revise my words accordingly.

* * *

Lesson #89: What you say is important—and how you say it is equally so.

* * *

Your voice's pace, tone, and volume are just as important as your content. It is often necessary to adjust your approach to the audience. You should always be polite and professional in front of an audience or an individual decision-maker, even if (s)he is informal to put you at ease. On the other hand, speaking at a seminar of peers permits you to be more informal and humorous. Speak clearly and avoid a monotone to avoid putting the audience to sleep. And remember what your mother said about "Please" and "Thank you."

Nonverbal communication is a natural weakness of mine, so I must always strive to be mindful of how I come across and adjust accordingly. One should maintain an open stance when standing to speak. Eye contact is necessary to show the other party you are speaking to them, without staring, of course. One should note the other person's nonverbal communications as well.

Also important is paying attention to the other party's behavior and body language to detect hidden meaning to their words. However, do not make the mistake of practicing reflective listening—that is, parroting back the exact words the other party says. Phrases like "I hear you say . . ." followed by a direct quote tells the person that you hear without acknowledging the merit of what they say, and in my experience is a real turnoff to decision-makers.

Objections and tough questions are sure to arise. Some preparation on your part is key to overcoming them. But even more important is to hear and understand the objections.

*   *   *

Lesson #90: You will learn more by listening than by speaking.

*   *   *

The art of active listening cannot be overestimated within a federal agency. So much is communicated informally and verbally that it is an essential skill to have. One must pay attention to what the other party is saying, ask questions to clarify your understanding, and rephrase when necessary. The other party can tell if you are really listening instead of thinking about what to say next.

This approach emphasizes for the listener concentrated focus, instant feedback, and related follow-up questions. Empathy with the speaker is more important than personal thoughts or emotions by the listener. We see this every day in medical counseling of potential life-and-death situations, police officers calming down domestic disturbances, and 911 operators handling fire call-ins or suicide threats. This showing of empathy is done to avoid conflict and misunderstandings, and also to build trust toward a satisfactory solution.

Coming hand-in-hand with active listening is the need for creativity. Most federal careers require to some degree the ability to sell your position to your supervisor. I was told early in my career by my manager, "The secret to this job is to identify the problem and develop prudent solutions." How true he was! The bureaucrat who engages in analytical work must frequently develop solutions to problems that arise in the course of agency performance. The more complicated the problem, the more imaginative the thinking must become.

* * *

Lesson #91: Perplexing problems demand creative solutions.

* * *

Many federal employees and contractors are analysts in a particular discipline. The analyst must fully identify the problem and its underlying issue(s), since frequently more than one issue is present. As stated before, it is then a wise idea to identify all the stakeholders in the outcome and their interests and motivators. Next comes brainstorming a list of possible solutions and evaluating each for its merits. This often requires heavy doses of creativity and research, calling on experts and past file folders as well as the Internet. Fact-finding is necessary to properly structure the problem to develop a prudent solution, as well as to identify any barriers or constraints to potential solutions. One must then discard those which are not feasible or even possible and compare those which remain to select the best option available. This decision must be documented, including reasons why other options were disregarded. Agreements with stakeholders and contingency arrangements may be necessary. Then comes the real trick—selling the solution.

To sell your position, you must first be confident in what you are selling. Your solution must be appropriate for the audience and of high value and acceptable cost. Once you have confidence in what you are selling, you will have confidence in yourself.

There are entire books written about business communication and salesmanship skills available at your local library and online. Here are a few ideas I have picked up over time:

- be positive and tactful;
- don't say "certainly" or "undoubtedly" if your position is disputable—instead say "it appears" or "if I'm not mistaken";
- reinforce the manager's interest by asking if your solution is helpful. This causes him/her to acknowledge value and could gain commitment to your solution;
- remain open to alternative ways to solve the problem;
- think before speaking; and
- understand the other person's interests and concerns.

PRIVACY

Before leaving the subject of communication, a few words on privacy are appropriate. The Privacy Act of 1974 (5 U.S.C. 552a) mandates agencies follow certain procedures and safeguards to collect, store, and disseminate personally identifiable information.[1] Protecting such information is essential to engender public trust in data collection and prevent identity theft. Agencies prescribe their own procedures for protecting such information, such as applying protective markings, encrypting internal e-mail, keeping data off Internet pages or share drives, and locking up hardcopy. These procedures will warn the individual against unauthorized information loss or sharing, browsing without authority, or leaving a workstation without protection. Any government employee who willfully discloses or obtains such information could be fined up to $5,000, and any contractor could be responsible for paying costs for replacement, theft protection, and possibly attorney's fees.

Within the context of privacy, a *record* is any item or collection of information about an individual that is maintained by an agency (e.g., criminal or employment history, education, financial transactions, and medical history). A record contains the individual's name and identifying number or symbol (including a fingerprint, photograph or voiceprint). When an agency contracts to design, develop, maintain, or operate a *system of records* (a group of records from which information is retrieved by the individual's name or identifying number or symbol) on individuals on behalf of the agency, then the contractors and their employees are considered employees of the agency in terms of Privacy Act criminal penalties. The system of records is deemed to be maintained (or collected, used or disseminated) by the agency and is subject to the Privacy Act. Agencies which fail to require that such contractor operations conform to the Act may be civilly liable to individuals who claim injury under the Act. The contract work statement specifically identifies the system of records on individuals and the design, development, or operational work to be performed. The solicitation will also make available any agency rules and regulations implementing the Act.

The *Freedom of Information Act*, or FOIA, generally provides any person with the statutory right, enforceable in court, to obtain access to government information in executive branch agency records. This right to access is limited when information is protected from disclosure by one of FOIA's statutory exemptions:[2]

- agency personnel practices;
- classified information;
- confidential commercial or financial information;
- interagency or intra-agency memoranda;

---

1. Lindner, 67.
2. FAR 24.2.

- law enforcement;
- personal and medical information pertaining to an individual; and
- trade secrets.

Personally Identifiable Identification (*PII*) is data about an individual that identifies or relates specifically to him or her (e.g., a Social Security number, age, home or office phone numbers, marital status, military rank or civilian grade, race, or salary). This includes any biometric, demographic, financial, medical, and personnel information. This data is not releasable. All releasable information is provided through the Federal Register, a requestor's visit to the archives with copy privileges, or mailing a copy to the requestor.

Chapter 12

Meetings and Presentations

Meetings are a constant feature of the federal work experience. *Meetings* involve two or more people who meet to exchange information verbally in order to achieve a goal or reach an agreement. I have worked in offices where managers met three times a day, and others where they met once a week. I worked in a position where I had to get three separate divisions to work together and had several meetings each day to facilitate meeting deadlines. My personal record is eight meetings in one day! Needless to say, meetings became a daily and pivotal part of my job.

Meetings can be done by telecon, phone, or videoconference, in a conference room, at a workstation or desk, in a hallway, or at the coffee mess or common area. However, courtesy to others should direct the meeting either toward an enclosed area such as a vacant room or else a quiet discussion on the telephone. It is not appropriate to disturb others through noisy conversations or clogged walkways. This is one of my pet peeves:

* * *

Lesson #92: Hallways are walkways, not meeting rooms.

* * *

Meetings can be misleading because they can give us a sense of accomplishment, when really all that is accomplished is deferring action to a later date, in effect "kicking the can down the road." Topics often lead to setting up a workgroup to do further research and develop options, often because nobody in the room has a good solution that everyone can agree on. Work groups also tend to delay decisions, which lead to the ultimate plethora of meetings and more meetings, further taking up time, and adding frustration for all. And inevitably, employees and managers attend meetings (or send duly assigned representatives) only to avoid being left out of the decision-making process and information flow.

*   *   *

Lesson #93: Invite only those who need to be there.

*   *   *

A formal meeting is called in advance to a select group of invitees. Common courtesy calls for attendees to respond to the invitation with either an acceptance or a polite decline. Make sure the date, time, and location are reflected prominently in the invitation. The host is responsible for securing the room through agency channels, which may require a request to a central office to schedule the room. Federal offices usually have limited conference room space, which is why many meetings are held at contractor facilities (where conference rooms tend to be more available).

An unusual aspect of federal meetings is that they are rarely held on Mondays, since so many people on compressed work schedules take that day off. Therefore, Tuesdays are meeting days in federal agencies. Auto traffic is much heavier on meeting days. It seems that in the Washington, D.C., area, accidents are down on Tuesdays—I surmise this is because people are concentrating on the traffic in order to get to work on time for their meetings. People also dress more professionally on meeting days. I once mentioned this to a clothing retailer I was visiting, and he responded, "Oh, is that why business is so quiet on Tuesdays?" Well yes, because everybody is in the office in meetings!

The host must also arrange in advance a list of hotels and restaurants in the area (if the meeting stretches past one day), and any coffee and pastries, which always seem to draw a larger crowd! It is also critical to arrange for any audiovisual aids such as videoconference or visual equipment.

*   *   *

Lesson #94: Practice using the equipment before the meeting.

*   *   *

Practice time for such equipment is always a wise idea to ensure familiarity with its operation. Most hosts and participants use a laptop, so be sure you practice getting the presentation on screen smoothly. If you use a projector, bring a spare light bulb because the projector will go dead just when you need it most. If you have remote offices calling in, make sure you know how to run the audio connection and have the proper phone number and password.

The host should check the room for sufficient lighting, table, and chairs. The room should be comfortable for everyone, so check the temperature control beforehand. Remember that a crowd of people generates heat, so turning up the temperature is a really bad idea!

The room should have enough power outlets for all table seats to charge their laptops. I cannot count how many meetings I have been to where multiple attendees were upset from the start because there were no power outlets for their ten-foot power cords to reach.

Large meetings may have two rows of chairs, one around the table and one along the walls. The table chairs are for the principals and decision-makers, while the wall chairs are for aides. These aides cannot just sit anywhere—they must sit behind their principal to consult with them (by whisper) during the meeting. Aides should know their place, and not speak out loud unless called upon. Consultants usually sit around the wall, too.

Have you ever seen a picture of the president convening a meeting in the White House? Look at the seating arrangement. The president always sits in the middle to ensure closeness to everyone and that all information funnels into the middle, not towards one end. If a decision-maker is running the meeting, (s)he should always sit in the middle on either side of the table. This also sends the message that the meeting is for discussion and sharing ideas collaboratively, not for dictatorial directives. On the other hand, this rule does not apply if the meeting is run by a facilitator with a number of equal-ranking officials; in this case, seating of the facilitator is based on such mundane aspects as access to audio-visual equipment. However, chairs should not be placed at the head of the table to allow everyone to see the screen or whiteboard.

If the meeting will last more than three hours or so, such as a training session, then coffee and snacks are appropriate. And yes, donuts and sweets are acceptable because they are comfort food, and everyone wants to be comfortable in a long training session. For a shorter meeting, however, food sends the wrong message: namely, that the meeting will run on and take up too much time.

The host should send all accepted attendees an agenda of the meeting about a week beforehand to provide advance notice of what will be discussed. This is especially true if key stakeholders and decision-makers will attend. Some proposed attendees may decide from the agenda that the meeting will not be worth their time, so this helps them to decide whether to attend. Others who are quite interested will use this notice to review their notes and in-house information on the anticipated topics so they can prepare for active participation.

* * *

Lesson #95: Start and end on time.

* * *

A meeting that starts late for whatever reason is off to a bad start. Remember that you are taking up other people's time and travel. Technical glitches should be rare (though they do happen at the worst possible times) because you have already checked the room and equipment. The meeting should never be delayed because an attendee is late unless that attendee is the sole decision maker invited and essential to the discussion of the topic. Nonetheless, tardiness should not normally be penalized, unless a supervisor is calling the meeting for subordinates.

Participants are also responsible for effective meetings. They should read any advance materials sent to them *before* leaving for the meeting (preferably including a copy on their laptop or tablet), arrive on time, keep an open mind as they listen to others, participate without taking over the meeting, and avoid conflict or raising their voices. If an extraneous topic is sidetracking conversation, schedule a separate meeting to discuss it. Optimal length is twenty to thirty minutes before interest lags, unless the subject is of great interest and intensive (such as a reorganization). If possible, sit within full view of the chairman or most senior official present. It usually helps to know everyone present if you are all sitting around a table (of course, this is not necessary if sitting in an auditorium) to understand their roles and responsibilities.

All attendees should put their cell phone on silent mode or else turn it off. Nobody should pull it out just because somebody sent them a message: it is rude and disrespectful to others. It is so annoying to a speaker to have their audience glance at their phones while trying to educate them.

Minutes are notes of what was discussed and resolved during the meeting. These minutes should list all attendees, and a sign-in sheet should be placed at the entrance door or else circulated at the beginning of the meeting. Minutes should not record every comment by every member, since many of them tend to deviate from the targeted topic. However, they should serve to remind members of what was discussed and notify other persons of interest what was decided or resolved. There is no prescribed format for minutes in federal government: the agency or program office decides the format. Official minutes are filed only for regulatory meetings or administrative law sessions. (I would send out the minutes on a government e-mail server, which made them official records but not formally filed.)

There is a difference of opinion over the level of detail within minutes. I participated in one working group whose minutes merely said, "A discussion was held regarding document formatting," without any further specifics. I personally found that to be useless and lacking much information, since document formatting would directly affect my work at the time. The chair of the committee was polite but did not feel it was appropriate to include any detail in the minutes, which led to frequent telephone calls and e-mail traffic regarding specific details.

When I ran a technical working group, we discussed many issues of a highly technical nature. Many comments raised additional aspects which I had never encountered before, which was not surprising because I insisted on bringing together people of greater technical expertise than I had, and I wanted to listen carefully and process what they said as they were saying it. I always learned a lot. Much of this knowledge would have been lost if I were busy writing it down. So I always brought along an assistant who served as a recording secretary to write down what was being said. This freed me to listen to every comment and actively participate in discussions without losing my train of thought by writing down notes. My assistant then typed up the notes and sent them to me in a couple of days. I then edited them, adding my own notes and recollections, and sent the minutes to our listserv about a week after the meeting. This process worked very well for all parties.

*   *   *

Lesson #96: Practice your tone and pace of speech before speaking.

*   *   *

It's not what you say that counts but how you say it. Do not be afraid to let your emotion and personality show. If the meeting gets heated, take time to calm down if you or anyone is angry. This time delay also helps to defuse any tense situation in a meeting.

It is also a good idea to occasionally ask if your information is on track and helpful to the audience. It does no good to blast through a twenty-minute presentation if the audience has lost interest after two minutes. Here again, overdoing it is a killer: don't stop after every point or slide to ask if this is what they want to hear. This behavior merely broadcasts lack of understanding about the purpose of the meeting. However, an approach that encourages continuous feedback may be necessary to gaining commitment.

I have often learned something during most of my presentations by hearing objections and asking questions about circumstances that I never anticipated. It also helps that audience members are smarter than me on the subject matter, since I usually learn quite a bit that I never thought of before. This approach will not only help to overcome adversarial reactions, but will prevent you from looking foolish and ill-prepared. Nobody wants to see a speaker look dumbfounded—it is a sure way to kill a presentation.

Action items should be assigned as they come up. This means an action tracker which lists each action, the responsible person, and due date. Frequently I have been the person who took on the responsibility, and the minutes so indicated. It is a good idea to summarize at the end of the meeting what has transpired and been decided on. The minutes should be sent to all attendees within a week of the meeting, along with the date/time/location of the next meeting. If you wish to permit feedback and corrections, then set deadlines for follow-up.

Everybody should be encouraged to participate, but don't single out someone who does not wish to talk. They might just be there as an observer to report back to their office what happened at the meeting, or they might be shy, or they might not be comfortable with their level of knowledge in the particular issue. Don't embarrass them by calling them out, although you must be mindful of people who call in and ask if any of them wish to add to the conversation.

*   *   *

Lesson #97: Shut down people who ramble or interrupt.

*   *   *

People who interrupt a speaker or other meeting participants are being rude. The host needs to curtail these interruptions to keep the meeting on task and tempers even. Chronic interrupters may escalate to bullying behavior. The chair should also ask speakers to describe or explain their positions to provide further information for all attendees, gently disagree when necessary by expressing it as a potential problem, build consensus by asking if anyone agrees with the proposal, and relieve tension when necessary.

For a meeting participant who rambles, the host can politely interrupt and ask them to get back to the main point. Or the host can gently interject with a summary of what they are saying and then say, "Moving forward . . ."

Leaving a meeting because it is truly a waste of your time is never easy to do. You will have to look at your watch and say, "Sorry, I have got to run for another meeting," and then get up and leave. Don't wait for permission, just go. Of course, don't do this if your meeting is chaired by someone in your chain of command. Yet, this is easier if the meeting is running beyond its allotted time.

Humor may be appropriate to keep the meeting flowing and defuse any tensions, but otherwise has no place in a formal meeting. Don't use it as a platform to tell the funny joke you heard that morning at the coffee mess or kitchen. Besides, you might offend someone and cause more headaches for yourself, especially if you need that person's concurrence to move forward with your agenda.

If somebody signals they want to talk but are being drowned out, call on them to speak. The facilitator can always redirect conversation in this manner. By the same token, a supervisor chairing a meeting can always call out someone who is not paying attention, especially by daydreaming. This actually happened in a meeting I attended when a team member yawned out loud. Our manager asked me to leave the room and a conversation ensued between manager and employee in my absence. This put me in an awkward position, but I quickly figured out that I was not the person in trouble. Two days later, the employee was terminated. I learned that there was more to the story than a simple yawn, and that his work performance was not up to par. Basically, he was a bad fit for the organization. Nonetheless, his behavior at the meeting was the catalyst for his dismissal.

At the end of the meeting, thank everyone for their time and participation.

Speaking skills for use in a meeting can be practiced by employee and decision-maker alike. Since most people these days have a limited attention span of twenty or thirty seconds, it is important to speak both concisely and clearly. A smile and good eye contact go a long way in grabbing someone's attention. After you have said your piece in that limited amount of time, stop. Let the other person digest what you have just said. If interested, (s)he will want to hear more. If not, politely move on. A firm handshake at the outset without gripping the other person in a vise is appropriate, and for goodness' sake don't flail your arms around like you are trying to take off in flight (a very annoying habit I have seen in people both young and old). A professional appearance, positive demeanor, and enthusiasm are also essential. Breathing deeply from the abdomen rather than shallowly from the chest is much better for your posture and voice. Be on time for the meeting and ask intelligent questions to further your knowledge and show interest to the leader.

There is much debate over whether regularly scheduled staff meetings are a good idea. Some say that they promote information flow with employees, while others say they are a big waste of time for everyone. I fall into the latter camp. As long as information is flowing freely, either through staff e-mail or unscheduled ad hoc meetings as necessary, I don't see where daily or weekly staff meetings do any good. They just become a habit without any real meaning.

I once worked on a large contract which had two separate work groups with their own leaders. One held staff meetings every day at 9 AM, where all team members spoke about what they would accomplish that day. It would often be

10 AM before they got a chance to face their client, so they lost about a quarter of their productive time due to a daily staff meeting. Therefore, sometimes they did not accomplish that which they had just said they would.

The other team leader (luckily, mine) held a daily staff meeting at 3 PM outside of the office in a setting with café tables and no chairs, requiring everyone to stand and share what they had accomplished that day. Since the meeting was near the end of the day and everyone just wanted to go home, these meetings were mercifully quick (often fifteen minutes) and sufficiently uncomfortable to speed them along. Of course, our meetings were more useful because they focused on results, not desires. Needless to say, our working group had a higher esprit d'corps, positive feeling of accomplishment, and longer evenings at home than the other team.

I did work in an office once where staff meetings were essential. All the managers sat along a row of windows (commonly known as "manager's row") while my entire branch sat in a closed office two hallways away. Space was limited for our large-sized division, so I had no opportunity to move in with them. So I adopted the policy of visiting them four times a day, twice in the morning and twice in the afternoon, to review individual work assignments and problems and pass along tidbits of information I had picked up. We did not need formal scheduled team meetings because I turned a negative seating situation into a positive means of communication.

Another way to address any problems with expectations seems to be setting ground rules at the very first staff meeting a new supervisor holds. Establish attendance policy of who does and does not attend these meetings, with expectations and roles for all attendees in terms of attendance and participation. Also to be addressed upfront are the objectives for the meetings (e.g., communication, discussion, problem-solving, etc.) with a clear agenda sent ahead of time to all attendees.

*   *   *

Lesson #98: Time is money.

*   *   *

Don't get me wrong: meetings are useful as a communications tool. They allow the manager to furnish employees with company news and initiatives, brainstorm ideas, and convey corporate plans and vision. They also provide an opportunity for employee socialization. However, many people see meetings as a grand waste of time.

Ironically, I learned a trick on this issue from my high school band teacher. When time was lost due to a substandard meeting, he would ask how many people were involved, how long the meeting ran (including prep time), do some quick calculating, then proudly announce how many human-hours were wasted in the effort. That approach works in a government setting as well as band practice!

Investigation by one group of academics found that senior managers spend about 23 hours a week in meetings, while non-supervisors and first-line managers spend maybe six hours per week in the conference room.[1] Because organizations are developing a flatter hierarchy to reduce overhead expense, employees are empowered to become more self-reliant, so meetings are becoming more important than ever to accomplish these goals. But the investigators also found that the more driven to achieve goals an employee becomes, the greater the level of dissatisfaction with meetings. Perhaps they see meetings as a grand waste of time that competes with job performance and productivity, and don't crave the socialization or job structure that less goal-driven employees desire.

Another survey further quantified the problem. After questioning nearly 200 senior managers across many industries, it determined that 71 percent found meetings to be inefficient and unproductive, and 65 percent found them to impede them from completing their own work.[2] More than 60 percent found that meetings do not promote thinking or bring the team any closer together.

Many employees love meetings because they can find out information on what is going on in the agency and then decide how it affects them personally and professionally. They are also good for spreading office gossip. And yet some people suffer from what one journalist calls the "Fear of Missing Out," while others celebrate the "Joy of Missing Out."[3] Some people are deathly afraid of missing something—anything—that happens in the office, no matter how trivial or unrelated to their own job. They often jump at the chance to join a working group to sharpen their skills, thirst for the newest computer technology (even while still in beta version), hope for managerial attention to enhance promotion potential, volunteer to travel anywhere at any time, or just socialize or change their daily duties or get a free drink. Those who fall into the Joy camp tend to be more pessimistic that the new project will succeed, decline to spend overtime in the office, tune out speakers in meetings in order to play a computer game (Solitaire is the game of choice for bored bureaucrats!), tolerate travel only to build up frequent flyer miles, and stay away from happy hour social gatherings on Fridays after work.[4]

---

1. Rogelberg et al., "The Science and Fiction of Meetings," *MIT Sloan Management Review*, 18–21.
2. Perlow et al., "Stop the Meeting Madness," *Harvard Business Review*, 62–69.
3. Bartleby (sic), "The Two Tribes of Working Life," *The Economist*, 55.
4. Unfortunately, civil servants are prohibited from keeping frequent flyer miles because it implies that they are unjustly benefitting from employment at the public trough. So much for that form of motivation!

*   *   *

Lesson #99: Become proficient with PowerPoint.

*   *   *

Formal presentations provide additional challenges to the speaker because informational materials need to be prepared. Learning the ins and outs of PowerPoint is essential to preparing slides for the attendees to follow with, though one should not expect them to be referred to after the meeting ends. They should be e-mailed to attendees before the meeting so they can be copied to laptops and tablets.

*   *   *

Lesson #100: Learn how to use your office printer and how to find and load paper.

*   *   *

Distribution of the slides in paper form as lap charts is discretionary for the speaker—it will make it easier for the attendees to follow. However, it creates more work for the speaker to print them out, so make sure the printer is properly working, load paper when it runs out (you do know how to load paper in the machine, don't you?), carry them to the meeting in bulk in a heavy briefcase, and ignore climate-friendly initiatives by slaughtering trees. In my experience, it is rarely worth the effort.

Your briefing slides should be set up in landscape format because most of us read from left to right rather than top to bottom. Each slide should bear a title in 24-point type, followed by information in bulleted format in 20-point type. If the bullets don't fit on one page, you either have too many bullets for the subject or else too broad a subject for one slide. Lengthy quotes and text usually do not go over well with the audience because they become too busy reading the slide to pay attention to what you are saying. Stay away from quotes, as a rule.

Simple graphs that are easily understood are helpful, but don't get carried away with how many charts you can develop. A colored background (such as gray or a light shade of green or blue) that is easy on the eyes is preferred. And for goodness' sake, proofread ahead of time to eliminate any typos! I have often run into people who proudly strut out of meetings because they "played gotcha" with the speaker by finding a typo, even though the meaning of the presentation is lost on them. Remember that you are the star of the show, not the slides—they are merely a tool to get your points across to the audience.

Chapter 13

Some Historical Case Studies

Now for some "war stories." These include lessons from actual historical events that I witnessed.

The first project I worked on for the Navy resulted from an operational problem, as so many defense projects do. Under agreement at that time with the government of Iceland, we deployed ships at their naval base in Keflavik. Remember that Iceland is near the Arctic Circle, so the windows often fogged up or contained frozen moisture. Crews standing watch in the bridge were unable to see through the glass and had to rely on officers standing on the bridge wing, exposed to the elements, shouting instructions to the navigator. This situation is "suboptimal" in military terms, meaning totally unacceptable. The solution devised by the Navy engineers was to design a "rotary window," which would necessitate cutting out a round section of the window and installing a heated circular inset with an arm like a windshield wiper. The arm would circle 360 degrees to clear a section of the window of all moisture, no matter how bad the weather. This would allow the bridge crew to see forward without stationing spotters outside in bad weather shouting their observations and hoping to be heard. The device was successfully engineered and produced. Today, I am pleased to say that it is in widespread use in naval vessels, oceangoing cargo vessels, and cruise ships. This is a classic example of the government developing a prudent solution to a real problem, benefitting multiple sectors of society.

Throughout the 1970s, the United States had a treaty with the Shah of Iran to provide him with jet fighters and to train his pilots in their use. Iran is located in a critical part of the world, in the oil-rich Middle East and near our archrival, the Soviet Union. It is also in the Arab world, which was encountering a rising tide of anti-Americanism. I was working in the office which provided contracting support for the Iranian government by bringing in field engineers from various aircraft and equipment manufacturers to provide on-site support and training to these pilots.

In 1979, the feeling of anti-Americanism reached a fever pitch as protests occurred across the country calling for the Shah's overthrow and establishment of an Islamic state. Our people were hearing from the on-site contractors that things were getting so bad that they began to fear for their lives. I saw many an employee run down the hallway daily to tell upper management what was going on and how conditions were deteriorating. Eventually, the Shah's government was toppled and the contracts terminated so that our engineers could get home safely. Luckily, the extraction process was well-managed and nobody was hurt.

This episode shows an important rule in action: we kept management informed on developing issues. And we made sure that they knew the bad news before they were blind-sided.

As a postscript, the fall of the Shah's government ended with 53 Americans taken hostage by the new Iranian regime for over a year until we had a change in presidents. Upon their release, they were flown to Washington and put up in a hotel literally across the street from where I worked. What a thrill it was to see them get off the bus, reunite with their families, and joyfully enter a luxury hotel with real beds for the first time in 15 months! When a local news reporter asked the hotel manager what he would do special for the now-ex-hostages, I remember him saying, "Whatever they want!"

In the mid-'80s, we went through a wave of procurement reform initiatives. This was occurring at a time when Senator Tom Harkin (Democrat, Iowa) was challenging the complexity of federal procurement regulations and asking why buying weapon systems couldn't be as easy as a farmer in his home state going downtown to buy a tractor. Well, it's not. A tractor is a standard commercial product with well-established pricing based on the features you want included. On the other hand, a weapon system is custom-built (farmers don't as a rule buy guided missiles to harvest their corn!) and must be priced out for each separate production run.

I wound up developing language for my boss, the Assistant Secretary of the Navy, to present to friendly congressmen and senators that was included in the Defense Procurement Reform Act of 1986. This meant exploiting an opportunity that was unexpected, but you have to be ready for any surprise development and jump in with both feet!

Among the many reform issues proposed by Congress that year was the idea that we should not do business with any company where at least five percent of the ownership was held by an entity from a state which supported terrorism. I thought it was a bad idea because it could restrict competition. At the very same time, Allis Chalmers, one of the three major tractor manufacturers in America, was being bought by Fiat Motor Company of Italy. No problem, right? Wrong. It turned out that Fiat was an internationally held firm, with over five percent ownership held by an entity based in Libya. This was also the time when the U.S. was angry at Libyan leader Muammar Gaddafi for sponsoring terrorism. So, the Reagan administration put out the word to financially combat terrorism supporters, and a member of Congress introduced this measure. After recommending objection to this proposal, I was told bluntly to support the measure by my Assistant Secretary. It was adopted that year and remains on the books. This was the only time when I gave bad advice to my boss, mainly because I failed to explore the political ramifications of the idea.

The most striking ethical crisis I saw in my career occurred in the mid-'80s. The FBI instigated a major investigation it called Operation Ill Wind to look into allegations of misconduct among both government and contractor officials.[1] It began with a market representative for Unisys, a major defense contractor, contacting an individual with another defense contractor with a promise to obtain bid information on one or more government contracts for his firm in exchange for cash. The individual then reported this inappropriate contact to NCIS and then the FBI, and the investigation began. He agreed to a wiretap on his telephone and elicited information from the marketer that was sufficient to establish probable cause and confront the individual. The marketer confessed and agreed to help the investigators, admittedly to save his own skin, and the scandal eventually opened up. Numerous indictments and guilty pleas followed. Ill Wind was the first time the FBI made widespread use of computer technology and wiretaps, and remains the largest defense procurement fraud case on record.

It also led to enacting the Procurement Integrity Act to prohibit any government official from releasing bid or source selection information prior to award, or from discussing employment with an offerer without disclosing the contact to a designated agency official.[2] This includes discussions with an agent or other intermediary of the company, not necessarily a company official. If such a contact is of interest, the official must disqualify him/herself from the procurement. It also requires of a designated official who participated in the procurement or program a "cooling off" period of one year after leaving federal employment before accepting employment with an offerer company.

---

1. Williams, "Unisys Corporation," The Center for Public Integrity.
2. 48 CFR 3.104.

168 *Chapter 13*

By the time it was over, the FBI estimates the total amount of fines and forfeitures at $622 million.[3] Roughly 60 people had been convicted or admitted guilt. I knew one of these people, a government attorney, whom I met with once or twice a month, who allegedly solicited a kickback by asking the contractor, "Hey, where's my cut?" He did not know that he was being recorded and was then confronted by NCIS investigators. He was a small fish in this corrupt pond, however, and the government was content with his resignation rather than wasting money on his prosecution. I thought I knew this guy, he was always a straight shooter with me, and I never suspected that he would be involved in this mess, much less actually solicit a kickback.

Three DoD officials went to prison as a result of accepting bribes and gratuities. Victor Cohen, Deputy Assistant Secretary of the Air Force, oversaw procurement of tactical military electronic systems and furnished Loral Systems with proprietary source selection information on a radar system procurement.[4] His conviction gave a black eye to the Air Force, which always prided itself on professionalism.

The other two convicts were Navy officials. Melvyn Paisley, Assistant Secretary of the Navy (Research and Engineering), was a distinguished fighter pilot in World War II and subsequent engineer in the aircraft industry. He was tried for accepting an excessively large severance package from Boeing, his former employer before accepting his Navy position, but was acquitted at his trial. Nonetheless, the scandal drove him from the government service. Four years later, he confessed to accepting bribes totaling six figures from both Unisys for an aircraft reconnaissance system and an Israeli partnership bidding on an aircraft procurement, and was sentenced to four years in prison. His Deputy Assistant Secretary, James Gaines, another former Boeing executive, took over his position until he too was convicted of accepting a gratuity (theater tickets and tires from, ironically, Paisley after his departure from the government) and spent six months in prison.[5] A subsequent reorganization by the Department of the Navy abolished their entire office, including the civil servants employed therein. Yes, innocent people lost their jobs because of their bosses' actions! I had worked with two of these individuals and was quite pleased with their help and so sorry to see them go involuntarily.

Two years later, I was on the team which analyzed overhead expenses and contract management functions at Unisys. Though we never uncovered anything illegal, our presence did put some heat on the contractor and led to the abrupt retirement of the senior civil servant overseeing their performance.

3. www.fbi.gov/history/famous-cases/operation-illwind.
4. DeLeon, *Thinking About Political Corruption*, 122.
5. *Seattle Times*, "Ex-Navy Official James Gaines Guilty of Accepting Gifts."

We never saw the fire but did uncover some smoke, so maybe something more was going on.

My first experience with the GAO came with an assignment to respond to their report regarding unfilled training billets for military personnel. GAO's sampling analysis showed numerous instances where commands would sign up enlisted personnel and officers for training, then cancel out with insufficient notice for the training activity to fill the vacancy. Worse, they found examples where the personnel just did not show up without any timely explanation. Although this is sometimes warranted as operational conditions dictate changes in priorities, it was clear from their investigation that this practice was routine within the military. Hence, training classes were not filled in many instances, costing money in terms of lost training opportunities. Their findings projected that the Navy had wasted $5 million per year in this practice.

My directive was to investigate this problem and find out how serious it was. My unofficial orders were to discredit the report and prove the situation really wasn't as bad as the GAO painted it. So I sent out data calls to our training center in Millington, Tennessee, to develop tuition figures for each course. Then I followed up with some commands to ascertain the reasons why people were not showing up for training. As expected, I found many late cancellations due to changing priorities. But I also found many military personnel who would change their plans voluntarily due to alleged work priorities which could not be officially verified. And of course, a number of personnel suddenly became too ill to travel, though they could miraculously commute to work.

Armed with this information, I created a spreadsheet to crunch numbers of dollars and failed attendees. I then created a briefing page demonstrating to my utter confidence that we had not wasted $5 million, as GAO had alleged. In fact, we had wasted $11 million!

When I briefed my division director, who was a member of the Senior Executive Service, he firmly said "Give me that!" and wrested the spreadsheet from me. After a couple of minutes of punching his calculator, he meekly said, "Okay. Send GAO a letter that we will try to do better next year."

The Air Force tried a different response. Their numbers were a little higher, just over $7 million as I recall. They responded by challenging GAO's sampling techniques and methodology of calculation, refusing to acknowledge any problem. Well, GAO could not sit still for that and dug deeper into the Air Force cancellations, leaving us alone. Their second investigation resulted in a finding of well over $12 million in lost training opportunities within the Air Force. I don't know how many go-rounds they had with the Air Force, who never did acknowledge a problem, but GAO was back the next year to assess another year of Air Force training experiences, but this time without looking at the Navy. We were off the hook.

I scored major points that day. Lessons learned: Be honest, don't lie. Do your homework and make sure your position is bulletproof. And don't deny a problem exists if it really does.

About the same time, the news broke that the Air Force had bought a hammer for $600. Future vice president Al Gore gave legs to this story by creating the Hammer Award to highlight wasteful DoD spending. In actuality, the hammer only cost $15; however, it was bought as part of a spare parts package for the airplane crew to make on-site repairs. When overhead costs were properly spread across all items procured under the contract, an additional $420 was added (as I recall), leading to a figure of $435. I have no clue how it grew to $600 in the public milieu, but I would guess that exaggeration had something to do with it.

This was not my program, thankfully, but I did know the auditor who worked on this review. She was adamant that proper accounting procedures were used to allocate overhead expenses and that there was nothing wrong with the bookkeeping. The public and the press did not agree. This proves that you must be aware of what the press will say, that there are critics around every corner, and that the bureaucrat and decision-maker alike must have their supporting documentation available for scrutiny.

I once served on the DoD Cost Principles Committee which drafted regulations governing cost allowances for contractors. Another member of the committee, a certified public accountant who was highly regarded in the business, introduced a case to recognize pension costs as a liability should a company be bought out or sold. His argument was that "accounting exactitude demanded" that such costs be so recognized. Backed by my in-house insurance and pension expert, I argued that this was not an issue of concern for the defense world, that it would only serve to reduce the sale price of these firms, and it would create a liability which we should not shoulder the cost of. I lost the battle on the regulatory level . . . until the Comptroller of DoD saw it. He killed the case instantly, buying my argument that we should not get involved with this issue. That represents the position of the government and corporate America today. This is why pensions are being superseded by 401(k) plans across the country.

As an afterword, the committee member who had championed this case was so angry at being overruled that he submitted his retirement papers and was gone within three weeks. We lost a well-respected civil servant, but he could not accept an adverse decision. Lesson learned: keep your ego in check and roll with the punches.

On the evening of August 1, 1990, Saddam Hussein ordered his Iraqi army to invade the sovereign nation of Kuwait. He claimed that he was merely exercising an ancient territorial right to annex a state of Iraq. The rest of the world denounced his action in what President George H.W. Bush called "naked aggression." That night, just four hours after the attack, one of the men I supported at work (along with a colleague) boarded an airplane in Washington and flew to Riyadh, Saudi Arabia, our ally. They became the first civil servants to respond to the invasion and arrive in the Arab world. What became known as Operation Desert Shield had begun and would later evolve into an offensive action known as Operation Desert Storm.

I was there at the beginning as we developed plans to respond to the Iraqi threat. We did not know at that moment how far Saddam Hussein would carry the fight. Would he be satisfied with annexing Kuwait, or would he move further? We knew that he had not hidden his desire to absorb Mecca, the holiest of cities in the Muslim world. Mecca is located in western Saudi Arabia near the Red Sea, so this meant he would need to traverse a great deal of Saudi Arabia to reach it. And right along that path of potential invasion lay King Khalid City, the cornerstone of Arab military strength and equipment storage. Could Hussein resist such a tempting target? We did not know.

One of the projects I worked on was to research and develop a classified system to maintain communications with soldiers deployed in a combat setting. This was a great idea—except that nobody approved its research until *after* Hussein had invaded Kuwait. The research company was ready to push the envelope, but everyone agreed that actual production and deployment was at least eighteen months away. Since our strategy was to accomplish our mission within six months, production was deferred until after the campaign.

Today, I am pleased to say that the technology we researched has been put to use by our soldiers on the ground in Afghanistan and Iraq. However, it also proves that you cannot wait until a war has begun to develop the tools to win. We always have to plan ahead for the next war even when we are mired in a current conflict. Research and development just cannot wait.

Another story from Operation Desert Shield features some rough sledding. I later supported another office that was involved in advanced development of military hardware. Once war broke out, the office sent three employees with their classified hardware to support the cause. They got off the plane in Riyadh, stood on the tarmac with their equipment . . . and just stood there! Nobody had thought to plan the logistics of their visit. They had to find a taxi cab, pack all their equipment in the trunk, figure out where they were supposed to go, and so forth. It must have been so embarrassing for them. Again, lesson learned: plan ahead.

I spent a number of years working on a program to develop an information system to automate the procurement function in the DoD. The office issued a draft solicitation which was universally criticized for its shortcomings by all parties, both government and industry. Since I was the "new kid on the block," I needed two months or so to convince the program manager that I had some level of capability. Then I assumed the responsibility of cleaning up the draft document to develop a final solicitation that would meet all criticisms and fulfill DoD and federal contracting requirements. Working hand-in-hand with an information systems engineer, I revised the technical specifications and some special provisions for the solicitation.

Then things got more complicated. The contracting officer and program manager were both so pleased with my efforts that I was told to take a crack at two harder problems, namely the functional specifications and a notional deployment schedule. The schedule was somewhat complicated because I had more than 1,000 sites to set up from the different services. DoD procurement operations are more geographically dispersed than you might think. For instance, the National Guard has at least one office in every state, more in larger states (California alone had six offices). At that time, every office had its own server, and nobody had developed "cloud computing" or remote processing and storage, so the software had to be deployed at every single site.

I was able to use input from all services and independent DoD agencies to craft a deployment schedule based on priority of both importance in operations and need to retire legacy systems. The latter was important because we were approaching the end of the millennium, when data fields routinely reserved only two digits to reflect the year, yet were programmed to do simple subtraction to determine available slack time. So "2000" would be written as "00," while "1901" would be "01." The difference in time would then be a negative 99 years, which was logically impossible and therefore caused the legacy program to lock up. Such systems either had to be reengineered or else retired. Hence the need to prioritize their retirement in the deployment schedule. It took some time, but I developed a rational schedule which passed muster with higher authorities.

The functional specifications were another problem. DoD had set up a team of users to develop their requirements, and they certainly turned it into quite a project. They wanted the system to do everything: procurement, travel requests and claims, personnel actions such as job applications and promotions, bonuses, e-mail, and so forth. In other words, they wanted a complete office suite embedded into one application. That was not about to happen, since nobody had or could build such a thing. Moreover, it would take up so much space on a local server that it could not even run within the given storage capacity. It was the classic case of a committee designing a mouse and coming up with an elephant!

I took the approach of focusing on only procurement operations, reduced the 700-plus requirements down to a manageable size of 400, eliminated the unrelated office needs that should be handled by other applications, and developed a set of requirements which was vetted by the committee and adopted with only one change (yes, I had forgotten one requirement). It became the basis for a successful solicitation, the first major commercial solicitation in DoD history.

The lessons learned here were to remain focused on the job at hand, stick to the scope of work, and maintain determination to complete the task within the allotted time. I kept the contracting officer regularly apprised on where I stood, satisfied them with my progress, and got the job done.

My parents and their generation remembered where they were and what they did when Pearl Harbor was attacked. My generation can remember where we were when President John Kennedy was assassinated (my school teacher ran out of the room in terror!). All of us can remember where we were and what happened during the attacks on 9/11. One of my neighbors lost a close friend in the World Trade Center towers. My father lost two business associates in the Pentagon who were meeting in a conference room, the very spot where the fuselage of the hijacked plane settled.

I was on Capitol Hill waiting for a congressional hearing to begin. They had a local news channel on the television, purely by coincidence, when the news broke that a plane had crashed into the World Trade Center. We all saw the first pictures of the smoke. Then the second plane hit. We were told that the starting time of the hearing would be delayed from 10 to 11 o'clock while Congress would hold an impromptu prayer session. Then one of the technicians began laying cable on the floor for the sound system for the hearing. I distinctly remember a committee staffer said to him, "I wouldn't do that just yet if I were you. This may not happen today."

Sure enough, just moments later the newscaster said, "We have just received a report that an airplane has crashed into the Pentagon." I instinctively grabbed my suit jacket and blurted out, "That's it. We are going to be chased out of here." Just three minutes later, they announced evacuation of all buildings on Capitol Hill and shutdown of all government offices in Washington. As we paraded outside in a very orderly fashion (everybody fully cooperated without any panic whatever), I was struck by two sights. First, I saw an Army officer in battle fatigues on the steps to ensure that the building was evacuated. Then I glanced to my right and saw the plume of smoke from the Pentagon. It brought home the image of war, not halfway around the planet or on a distant Pacific island—but right here on the mainland of the United States!

We were herded onto the subway, rode out of Washington to the Virginia side of the Potomac, then waited—and waited—and waited some more—for a train to take us due west. My car was parked in a garage to the south, on the other side of the Pentagon, which was closed to subway traffic. So I could not get to my car. I rode the only train that I could get, finally got cell phone service shortly before arriving at the last stop on the line outside the Beltway, because the satellite was flooded with phone connections. I called my wife (everyone in such a crisis makes their first call to their family), who picked me up and drove me to get my car out of the parking garage and go home.

The lesson here is just what the Boy Scouts preach: be prepared. Have an escape plan. Be flexible and able to adjust your actions to the situation.

I started my first tour at FEMA about one year after Hurricane Katrina devastated New Orleans and nearby areas of the Gulf Coast. Truly "The Storm of the Century," Katrina caused at least $80 billion (maybe $150 billion) worth of damage to the Alabama and Mississippi coastlines, the entire state of Louisiana, the Ohio Valley, and even into Ontario. Although President George W. Bush initially stood by his agency in their response efforts, it soon became clear that FEMA was unable to meet the heavy level of reaction required of this disaster.

By the time I came aboard a year later to help fix the procurement operation which had been largely inadequate in the ensuing months, nearly every senior official in the agency had been replaced. I remember one official, a career civil servant who was on vacation on the beach in Cancún when the hurricane struck and refused to give up her beach seat to return early. She was thoroughly uncooperative to us and to her immediate supervisor, rejected a buyout offer, and slowed down, if not discouraged, any cooperation from her staff. I don't recall ever dealing with a government executive who was so resistant to meeting with anybody, even her own chain of management. Months later, she was called into a meeting with senior FEMA management. I have no clue what transpired in that meeting, whether they sweetened the offer or threatened her, but she did leave within a few days.

The new director of FEMA was David Paulison, who was a nonpartisan official at a time when nonpartisanship was badly needed. He had been a firefighter in Miami and rose through the ranks to become chief. He then retired to take over the U.S. Fire Administration, which has a training facility in Emmitsburg, Maryland, to train first responders and firefighters from smaller fire departments which do not have the resources to perform their own training. I visited this facility several times and was struck by its professionalism, even on a tight budget. Paulison also had run the Preparedness Division of FEMA and issued guidance on how citizens should prepare for natural emergencies and terrorist attacks. I thought he did a fantastic job in resolving a number of inefficiencies in the agency.

My year in that tour of duty required a great deal of meetings and handholding among the Information Systems, Recovery, and Procurement divisions. Progress was measured by accomplishing literally one step on one action at one time. Many purchase requests were lost in the system—often to dead-letter or incorrectly addressed e-mail boxes. We were ultimately able to locate or reinitiate every single procurement action and get them awarded on time. In my final week on the job, I actually got all three divisions to talk to each other, thereby breaking down the stovepipes that had permeated the agency up to that time. That was quite a success story!

One lesson learned at FEMA was to establish and maintain communications channels on all levels. I had to constantly run around and tactfully consult with people who were too busy or otherwise uninterested in talking to me. Another lesson was perseverance: investigating every open item and digging until we got resolution.

When I served as legislative liaison for the Assistant Secretary of the Navy, I earned the opportunity to meet with several well-known senators (my workload was such that I only met a couple of representatives). Hence, some personal remembrances seem fitting to wrap up this book.

John McCain (Republican, Arizona) may be the best-known senator I ever met. I must say that the man we saw in the 2008 presidential campaign was the real John McCain. He was very passionate about certain subjects, such as defense spending and the treatment of prisoners of war, and woefully unknowing about others, such as the economy. I seem to recall that he uncovered the Druyan scandal. He was a very honest and personable man and very pleasant to work with.

Bob Smith (Republican, New Hampshire) was a large man, built like a professional linebacker, who had served in Vietnam. He was also a pleasure to see in action, very considerate to everyone, and always seemed to have his "ducks in a row." Though I'm nonpartisan due to my job, I was sorry to see him defeated for re-election.

Personalities differ among senators, though that is not necessarily a bad thing. Daniel Patrick Moynihan (Democrat, New York) was the finest gentleman I ever met. Very friendly to perfect strangers, he was a very caring man and well polished in both appearance and demeanor. In contrast, Daniel Inouye (Democrat, Hawaii) was very detail-oriented and focused on the job at hand. He tolerated no levity or humor, but rather was emotionally and mentally on the job every minute of the workday to identify waste and abuse.

The only time I met Brock Adams (Democrat, Washington) was after a story broke about allegations of sexual misconduct from several women. I met a broken man who seemed afraid of everyone he met, and he ultimately declined to stand for reelection. He reflected the physical and behavioral toll on a public figure once an embarrassing disclosure is revealed. He had served many years in Washington as a representative, Secretary of Transportation, and senator, and was truly a loss.

I also met one or two senators who reinforced the stereotype of partisan politicians who would not hesitate to utter a smart-aleck phrase to attack someone of a different opinion. In my experience, they are in the minority, so I will not dignify them with any further discussion.

My most curious Senate story involves Jesse Helms (Republican, North Carolina), who also had a reputation of partisanship. He was the ranking minority member (at that time, the Democrats controlled the Senate) on a committee with the usual two sets of staff members, one set majority and one set minority. On this particular day of hearings, the minority staff gave a report on a particular issue which was perhaps the worst presentation I ever sat through. Their numbers were easily refuted under examination by the majority staff members and any sort of simplistic mathematical analysis by the audience. Their conclusions were largely based on suppositions, not facts. While these fools were sweating in public, Senator Helms sat off to the side, literally laughing aloud with the audience. It could only be classified as a show of buffoonery. This hearing occurred on a Friday. The following Wednesday, Helms fired the entire minority staff. All of them! As a public servant, I would have to applaud his decision. They were hopelessly inept and partisan without any regard for the facts and certainly did no service for country or political party.

I had the pleasure of meeting two presidents, Jimmy Carter and George H.W. Bush (when he was vice president), both gentlemen and quite gregarious. I also met two cabinet members. Caspar Weinberger (Secretary of Defense under President Ronald Reagan) was very serious and focused on work, quite like Senator Inouye, and certainly dedicated to the mission. Every interaction and meeting with him was 100 percent business. Edwin Meese (Reagan's Attorney General) had more personality and maintained high standards of performance and interrelationships, and was far easier to talk to. He did expect high-quality briefings, however, and personally complimented me (then a youngster in the business) for doing a good and professional presentation. He sure boosted my self-confidence!

*   *   *

I close this book with one last case observation. On the 9/11 air attack on the Pentagon, 125 workers at the Pentagon lost their lives. The survivors moved out of the massive building in an orderly fashion as if in a fire drill, only to discover upon exit the explosion and scope of the attack. The Secretary of Defense, Donald Rumsfeld, ran to the crash site, quickly surveyed the damage, and pitched in to help with the injured.[6] Many other workers helped out that day, even though some of them were themselves injured.

---

6. Goldberg et al., *Pentagon 9/11*, 129.

The building was closed down the rest of the day, only to reopen the next morning. Military and civilian alike, employees streamed back into one part of the building that morning while firefighters were still putting out the fire in another part. I heard several of these workers say at the time that they came back because they felt it their duty to do so, that the nation was under attack and they would do their best to respond. Of course, some needed time to recover, while others had lost their work offices to the explosion. Eventually, they all came back.

Colleagues had died. Friends had perished. Fear ripped through their emotions. Yet they came back.

These military, civil servants, and contractors showed dedication to their task, to serve the nation and conduct the People's Business. This is what working for the federal government is all about.

Bibliography

PUBLISHED WORKS

Augustine, Norman R. *Augustine's Laws*. Reston, Virginia: American Institute of Astronautics and Aeronautics, 1984. Augustine was a DoD official and later president of Martin Marietta Corporation, now part of Lockheed.

Bartleby (sic). "The Two Tribes of Working Life." *The Economist*. February 2, 2019.

Bur, Jessie. "Security Clearance Agency Gets a New Name, Same Priorities." *Federal Times.* June 24, 2019. Retrieved September 23, 2019, from www.federaltimes.com/management/2019/06/24/security-clearance-agency-gets-a-new-name-same-priorities.

Bureau of Labor Statistics. "Working for the Federal Government: Part I." Washington, D.C.: Department of Labor, March 25, 2019. Retrieved August 3, 2019 from https://fas.org/sgp/crs/misc/R43590.pdf.

Cohen, Richard E., and James A. Barnes. *The Almanac of American Politics* (2018). Arlington, Virginia: Columbia Books, Inc., 2018. This resource includes information on every senator and representative and their respective district and state. It does not, however, include information on staff members.

Congressional Research Service. "Federal Workforce Statistics Sources: OPM and OMB." Washington, D.C.: Congressional Research Service, March 25, 2019.

Crosby, Olivia. "How to Get a Job in the Federal Government." *Occupational Outlook Quarterly* (Summer 2004). Retrieved March 5, 2019, from www.bls.gov/careeroutlook/2004/summer/art01.pdf. Crosby works for the Bureau of Labor Statistics.

Defense Acquisition University. *PGI Procedures, Guidance and Information*. Available online at https://www.dau.mil/tools/dag. This is a critical and comprehensive resource for acquisition, cost estimating, and program management within the Defense community.

DeLeon, Peter. *Thinking About Political Corruption*. New York: Routledge, 2015. DeLeon was a Professor of Public Policy at the University of Colorado, Denver.

Department of Defense. "About the Department of Defense." Retrieved September 3, 2019, from https://archive.defense.gov/about.

Department of Defense Public Affairs. "Our Story." Washington, D.C.: Department of Defense, 2019. Retrieved March 9, 2019, from https://www.defense.gov/Our -Story.

Department of Energy. "Architectural and Transportation Barriers Compliance Board Electronic and Information Technology (EIT) Accessibility Standards." Washington, D.C.: Department of Energy, June 2005.

Dorling Kindersley Publishing Staff. *Managing Your Boss*. London: Dorling Kindersley Publishing, Inc., 2003.

Drury, Horace Buckwalter. "Scientific Management: A History and Criticism." *Studies in History, Economics and Public Law* LVX, no. 2. New York: Columbia University, 1918. Drury taught economics and sociology at Ohio State University and industrial organization at the University of California.

Executive Order 12333. "United States Intelligence Activities." Washington, D.C.: Federal Register, December 8, 1981.

Executive Order 12968. "Access to Classified Information." Washington, D.C.: The White House, August 4, 1995.

Executive Order 13869. "Transferring Responsibility for Background Investigations to the Department of Defense." Washington, D.C.: The White House, April 24, 2019.

Federal Acquisition Regulatory Council. *Federal Acquisition Regulation*. Washington, D. C.: Government Printing Office, 2005. FAR is also printed in the Code of Federal Regulations, Title 48, Chapter 1, and available online at www.acquisition .gov/browsefar. This is the bible of federal contracting and a necessary reference book for all practitioners.

General Services Administration. "How the Supreme Court Works." Retrieved August 16, 2019, from https://www.usa.gov/branches-of-government#item-213376.

———. "SF-86 Questionnaire for National Security Positions." Washington, D.C.: Office of Personnel Management, December 2010.

Goldberg, Alfred, et al. *Pentagon 9/11*. Washington, D.C.: Office of the Secretary of Defense, 2007. Retrieved October 9, 2019 from https://www.history.navy.mil/re search/library/online-reading-room/title-list-alphabetically/p/pentagon-9-11-foot notes.html#VI.

Government Printing Office. *United States Reports*. Washington, D.C.: Government Printing Office, 2016.

Headquarters, Department of the Army. "Field Manual 6-0: Mission Command: Command and Control of Army Forces, Appendix C Staff Organization and Staff Officers." Washington, D.C.: Department of the Army, August 11, 2003. Retrieved May 11, 2019, from https://www.globalsecurity.org/military/library/policy/army/ fm/6-0/appc.htm.

———. "Field Manual 22-100: Army Leadership—Be, Know, Do." Washington, D.C.: Department of the Army, August 31, 1999.

Hegarty, Christopher, and Philip Goldberg. *How to Manage Your Supervisor*. Novato, California: New World Library, 1982. Hegarty is a management consultant and Goldberg is a spiritual counselor, both based in California.

Katz, Eric. "Agencies Paid Federal Employees $3.7 Billion Not to Work During Recent Shutdowns." *Government Executive*. September 17, 2019. Retrieved September 18, 2019, from https://www.govexec.com/pay-benefits/2019/09/agencies-paid-federal-employees-37-billion-not-work-during-recent-shutdowns/159936/.

Legislative Branch Capacity Working Group. www.legbranch.org/2016-6-17-how-many-congressional-staff-are-there. Retrieved February 26, 2019.

Leung, Rebecca. "Cashing In for Profit?" CBS News, January 4, 2005. Retrieved September 12, 2019, from www.cbsnews.com.

Library of Congress. "Official US Government Executive Web Sites." Retrieved August 18, 2019, from www.loc.gov/rr/news/fedgov.html.

Lindner, Dan. *A Guide to Federal Contracting: Principles and Practices*. Lanham, Maryland: Bernan Press, 2017.

Marks, Joseph. "OPM Is Still Far Behind on Data Protection Three Years After Devastating Breach." *Nextgov*. November 18, 2018. Retrieved April 26, 2019, from www.nextgov.com/cybersecurity/2018/11/opm-still-far-behind-data-protection-three-years-after-devastating-breach/152804.

McGregor, Douglas. *The Human Side of Enterprise.* New York: McGraw-Hill Companies, 2006.

Meredith, Jack R., Scott M. Shafer, Samuel J. Mantel, Jr., and Margaret M. Sutton. *Project Management in Practice*. Hoboken: John Wiley & Sons, 2017. Meredith was an engineer on several space programs and later a professor of management at Wake Forest University. He acknowledged several consultants who helped write this book.

Montesquieu, Charles-Louis de Secondat, Baron de La Brède et de. *Complete Works, Vol. 1 (The Spirit of Laws)*. Book XI Chapter VI. Retrieved February 27, 2019, from https://oll.libertyfund.org/titles/montesquieu-complete-works-vol-1-the-spirit-of-laws#lf0171-01_label_786.

National Academy of Sciences. "The Polygraph and Lie Detection." Washington, D.C.: National Academies Press, 2003. Retrieved March 21, 2019, from https://www.nap.edu/read/10420/chapter/1.

National Institute of Standards and Technology. "Federal Information Processing Standards Publication (FIPS PUB) Number 201, Personal Identity Verification of Federal Employees and Contractors." Gaithersburg, Maryland: National Institute of Standards and Technology, 2013.

Neal, Jeff. "Government Hiring Young People Continues to Be Terrible." May 1, 2019. Retrieved May 14, 2019, from https://chiefhro.com/. Neal formerly served as Chief Human Capital Officer for the Department of Homeland Security and Chief Human Resources Officer for the Defense Logistics Agency. Neal ran the human resources department for Defense Logistics Agency and Department of Homeland Security.

———. "Where Have All the Classifiers Gone?" Retrieved May 22, 2019, from https://www.fedsmith.com/2019/06/06/where-have-all-classifiers-gone.

The New York Times, August 14, 1986, B6.

Nierenberg, Gerard I. *Fundamentals of Negotiating*. Boston: Dutton, 2002. Nierenberg was a lawyer and consultant on business relationships and negotiations.

Office of the Director of National Intelligence. "Security Executive Agent Directive 4, National Security Adjudicative Guidelines." Washington, D.C.: Office of the Director of National Intelligence, June 8, 2017. Retrieved March 26, 2019, from http://ogc.osd.mil/doha/SEAD4_20170608.pdf.

Office of the Federal Register. *United States Statutes at Large*. Washington, D.C.: Government Printing Office, 2018. This is the repository for all federal laws.

Office of the Federal Register. *The U.S. Government Manual* (2017). Washington, D.C.: Government Printing Office, 2017. This manual describes agencies and key officials in the executive branch. The legislative branch section contains information about the roles of the House, Senate, Library of Congress, and Congressional Budget Office.

Office of the Law Revision Council, House of Representatives. *United States Code*. Washington, D.C.: Government Printing Office, 2012. This is the repository for all federal regulations.

Office of Management and Budget. "OMB Guidance M-05-24, Implementation of Homeland Security Presidential Directive (HSPD) 12-Policy for a Common Identification Standard for Federal Employees and Contractors." Washington, D.C.: Office of Management and Budget, August 5, 2005.

Office of Personnel Management. "The Security Clearance and Investigation Process." Washington, D.C.: Office of Personnel Management, undated. Retrieved October 17, 2019, from www.brac.maryland.gov/documents/security percent20 clearancepercent20101percent20pppercent20presentation.pdf.

———. "The Security Clearance and Investigation Process." Retrieved February 28, 2019, from www.opm.gov.

———. "Status of Telework in the Federal Government: Report to Congress, Fiscal Year 2017." Washington, D.C.: Office of Personnel Management, January 2019. Retrieved from www.telework.gov/reports-studies/reports-to-congress/2018 -report-to-congress.pdf.

Ogrysko, Nicole. "Federal Contractors Describe 'Insanity and Uncertainty' during Government Shutdown." *Federal News Network*, May 7, 2019. Retrieved May 8, 2019, from https://federalnewsnetwork.com/government-shutdown/2019/05/federal -contractors-describe-insanity-and-uncertainty-during-government-shutdown.

Perlow, Leslie A., Constance Noonan Hadley, and Eunice Eun. "Stop the Meeting Madness." *Harvard Business Review* (July–August 2017). Perlow is a Professor of leadership at Harvard, Hadley lectures on organizational behavior at Boston University, and Eun is a Professor of Philosophy at Yale University.

Polydys, Mary Linda, and Stan Wisseman. *Software Assurance in Acquisition: Mitigating Risks to the Enterprise*. Washington, D.C.: National Defense University (Information Resources Management College), February 2009. Wisseman is a security strategist for information systems. Polydys teaches acquisitions and data management for the Department at the Information Resources Management College at the National Defense University.

Priest, Dana, and William M. Arkin. "A Hidden World, Growing beyond Control." *Washington Post, July 19, 2010.*

Purves, Lloyd. *Secrets of Personal Command Power*. West Nyack, New York: Parker Publishing Co., 1981.

Roberts, Wess. *Leadership Secrets of Attila the Hun.* New York: Grand Central Publishing, 1990. Roberts has been a professor and business consultant, based in Utah.

Roesch, Roberta. *Smart Talk: The Art of Savvy Business Conversation.* New York: AMACOM, 1989. Roesch was a prolific writer specializing in women's issues.

Rogelberg, Steven G., Cliff Scott, and John Kello. "The Science and Fiction of Meetings." *MIT Sloan Management Review* (Winter 2007). Steven G. Rogelberg is a professor of organizational science and psychology at the University of North Carolina, Charlotte. Cliff Scott is an assistant professor of organizational science and communication studies at the University of North Carolina, Charlotte. John Kello is a professor of psychology at Davidson College in Davidson, North Carolina.

Rosenberg, Yuval. "Trump Administration Asks for $81.1 Billion Black Budget, the Largest Ever." *The Fiscal Times*, February 28, 2018. Retrieved August 1, 2019, from www.thefiscaltimes.com/2018/02/28/Trump-Administration-Asks-811-Billion-Black-Budget-Largest-Ever.

Santayana, George. *Reason in Common Sense.* London: Constable, 1905. This book was written during his time at Harvard University. He later became known as a cultural critic and pragmatist.

Seattle Times. "Ex-Navy Official James Gaines Guilty Of Accepting Gifts." March 8, 1991. Retrieved May 28, 2019, from http://community.seattletimes.nwsource.com/archive/?date=19920308&slug=1479915.

U.S. Census Bureau. "Apportionment of the U.S. House of Representatives Based on the 2010 Census." Washington, D.C.: Department of Commerce, 2011. Retrieved August 20, 2019, from www.census.gov/history/img/2010apportionment-map.gif.

———. "US States—Ranked by Population 2019." Washington, D.C.: Department of Commerce, 2011. Retrieved August 20, 2019, from http://worldpopulationreview.com/states/.

United States Constitution, 1787. The document that provides the foundation for our federal government.

United States Court of Federal Claims. "Frequently Asked Questions." Retrieved August 16, 2019, from www.uscfc.uscourts.gov/faqs.

United States Senate Permanent Subcommittee on Investigations. "The True Cost of Government Shutdowns." Washington D.C.: Government Printing Office, September 17, 2019.

Vilorio, Dennis. "Working for the Federal Government: Part 2." Washington, D.C.: Bureau of Labor Statistics, November 2014. Retrieved May 7, 2019, from https://www.bls.gov/careeroutlook/2014/article/how-to-get-a-federal-job.htm. Vilorio is an economist in the Office of Occupational Statistics and Employment Projections, BLS.

Williams, Brooke. "Unisys Corporation." Washington, D.C.: The Center for Public Integrity. https://web.archive.org/web/20071215105158/http://www.publicintegrity.org/wow/bio.aspx?act=pro&ddlC=59. Retrieved May 28, 2019. Note that this report is no longer active and was retrieved from the Wayback Machine at https://archive.org/web.

Zengerle, Patricia, and Megan Cassella. "Estimate of Americans Hit by Government Personnel Data Hack Skyrockets." Reuters, July 9, 2015.

WEBSITES

http://fedcas.com/wp-content/uploads/2012/05/Federal-Suitability-Security-Clearance-Chart.pdf
www.military.com
www.ssa.gov
www.tsp.gov
www.usajobs.com
www.dau.mil/tools/dag
www.defense.gov/Our-Story
https://godefense.cpms.osd.mil/loan_forgiveness.aspx
https://gogovernment.org
https://nbib.opm.gov/e-qip-background-investigations/#url=Quick-Reference-Guide
www.fbi.gov/history/famous-cases/operation-illwind. Retrieved May 6, 2019
www.federalnewsnetwork.com
www.military.com/military-transition/employment-and-career-planning/work-for-the-dod.html
www.nist.gov/itl/itl-publications/federal-information-processing-standards-fips
www.opm.gov/combined-federal-campaign
www.opm.gov/healthcare-insurance/healthcare/
www.opm.gov/healthcare-insurance/life-insurance/
www.opm.gov/healthcare-insurance/long-term-care/
www.opm.gov/openseason
www.opm.gov/policy-data-oversight/pay-leave/salaries-wages/#url=2019
www.whitehouse.gov/omb/

Index

Adams, Brock, 175

Agencies, U.S.: within DoD, 73–74, 74n3; executive orders on, 11; regulations by, 11; shutdown of federal, 16–17, 16nn23–24; types of, 30–33

Alaska, 5, 5n9

annual leave, 41–42

Anti-Deficiency Act, 16–17

appropriation bills: budgets with, 14–15; presidential veto of, 15; types of, 14–15

Architect of the Capital, 7

Army Field Manual 22-100, 99–100

background investigations: by contractor work force, 84; by Department of State, 84n15; by Department of Treasury, 84n15; by DoD, 84n15; by FBI, 84n15; by Homeland Security, 84n15; by National Background Investigations Bureau, 84–85, 84n15; as Single or Full Scope, 86

Beltway, 12

benefits: annual leave in, 41–42; bonuses in, 43; contractor work force and, 96; cost-of-living increases as, 40–41, 40n8; upon death, 47, 47n17, 71, 71n8; for disabilities, 3, 29, 65; evaluations and, 37, 42–43, 57n4, 87; family-friendly programs in, 45; Federal Employee Health Benefits program as, 45–46; health, 45–46, 46n14, 47, 47nn16–17; OFPP and health, 46, 46n15; OPM on salaries, 41; sick leave in, 41; telecommuting in, 43–45, 96–97, 96n7

bonuses, 43; earned, 41, 133; relocation, 45; retirement, 62, 67–68

Botanic Garden (U.S.), 7

bribes, 111, 167–68

budgets: Anti-Deficiency Act on, 16–17; apportionment and allotment of, 15–16; authorization and appropriation on, 14–15; CBO and annual, 7; civil servants collective bargaining and, 39; congressional debate on, 13, 13n22; Constitution on, 13, 13n21; continuing resolution for, 16; DoD budget and, 79; DoD spending and, 169–70; GAO and, 8; of intelligence and military, 79; legislative resolutions on, 13; OMB managing federal, 12–13, 91, 91n2; as planning or compliance tool, 16; submission process of, 12–13; types of spending in, 14–15

About the Author

Dan Lindner possesses 40 years of experience in federal acquisition and program management for the Departments of Defense and Homeland Security. He was a long-time contracting officer for the U.S. Navy and is well-versed in federal acquisition policy and procurement regulations. He has chaired review panels and study teams, negotiated contracts for major weapons system components, worked daily with administrative contracting officers, established a remote buying office, and served as a Small and Disadvantaged Business Utilization Specialist. As a staff aide to the Assistant Secretary of the Navy, he conducted personal briefings on pending congressional issues affecting defense acquisition and co-authored the Procurement Reform Act of 1986. Dan also established and chaired the Environmental Committee for Defense Acquisition Regulatory (DAR) Council, and was a member of the Cost Principles Committee, gaining expertise with Cost Accounting Standards. He also served as action officer for technical requirements, electronic commerce, and information systems security for a major Defense information system.

Dan also has a lengthy career in the private sector, working closely with technical and acquisition clients to define business needs and product requirements, counseling program managers and contracting officers to develop effective strategies, and helping to develop winning proposals. He also served as vice president for Mindcorp, Inc., a small business which furnished program management support to both federal and commercial clients.

In academia, Dan was an instructor for both the Navy Office of Human Services and Fairfax County (Virginia) Adult Education to develop and teach newly hired employees and acquisition professionals about procurement basics. He has developed and delivered presentations in national conventions and corporate meetings on Contract Administration, Network Security, and Portfolio Management. Dan wrote *A Guide to Federal Contracting:*

Principles and Practices to cover federal contracting across all departments and agencies and *A Guide to Defense Contracting: Principles and Practices* (both published by Bernan Press) to address contracting with the Department of Defense. He has written numerous monographs on defense acquisition, baseball, information technology, and travel.

Dan has been cited over ten times by Marquis and International Who's Who of America, Information Technology, Science and Engineering, and the World. He earned five Navy Performance Awards and the Director of Defense Procurement Award for Innovation in Procurement. He has earned several professional designations over time, including Certified Professional Contracts Manager, Project Management Professional, Level III Certification under the Defense Acquisition Workforce Improvement Act, Certified Information Systems Manager, and Certified in Risk and Information Systems Control.

Dan earned his Bachelor of Arts degree in both Government and Economics from Lehigh University, and an M.B.A. from George Washington University. He was cited as an Honors Graduate from both schools. He resides with his family in Virginia.